D1173777

WOMEN WHO RULED

10
ND1460
.W65
W66
2002

SCHOOL OF THE MUSEUM
OF FINE ARTS - BOSTON

WOMEN WHO RULED

Queens, Goddesses, Amazons
in Renaissance and Baroque Art

Annette Dixon, Editor

MERRELL

in association with

THE UNIVERSITY OF MICHIGAN MUSEUM OF ART

First published 2002 by
Merrell Publishers Limited
42 Southwark Street
London SE1 1UN

in association with

The University of Michigan Museum of Art
525 S. State Street
Ann Arbor, Michigan 48109-1354

Published on the occasion of the exhibition
Women Who Ruled: Queens, Goddesses, Amazons 1500–1650

EXHIBITION ITINERARY
The University of Michigan Museum of Art, Ann Arbor MI
February 17 – May 5, 2002

Davis Museum and Cultural Center, Wellesley College,
Wellesley MA
September 14 – December 8, 2002

Ford Motor Company

This publication and the accompanying exhibition are made
possible by Ford Motor Company.

Additional support has been provided by the Samuel H. Kress
Foundation, the National Endowment for the Arts, the
University of Michigan Office of the Provost, the Friends of the
Museum of Art, and a generous anonymous donor.

Distributed in the USA by Rizzoli International Publications,
Inc. through St. Martin's Press, 175 Fifth Avenue, New York,
NY 10010

© The Regents of the University of Michigan 2002

All rights reserved. No part of this publication may be
reproduced, stored in a retrieval system or transmitted
in any form or by any means, electronic, mechanical,
photocopying, recording or otherwise, without prior
permission in writing from the publishers.

Library of Congress Control Number 2001096065

Dixon Annette
    Women who ruled: queens, goddesses, Amazons in
    Renaissance and Baroque art
    1. Arts, Renaissance – Europe 2. Arts, Baroque – Europe
    3. Women in art 4. Queens in art
    I. Title
    700.4'52042'094'09031

ISBN 1 85894 166 0

Produced by Merrell Publishers Limited
Edited by Mary Ore
Designed by Matthew Hervey
Printed and bound in Italy

REGENTS OF THE UNIVERSITY OF MICHIGAN
David A. Brandon, Ann Arbor
Laurence B. Deitch, Bingham Farms
Daniel D. Horning, Grand Haven
Olivia P. Maynard, Goodrich
Rebecca McGowan, Ann Arbor
Andrea Fischer Newman, Ann Arbor
S. Martin Taylor, Grosse Pointe Farms
Katherine E. White, Ann Arbor
B. Joseph White, ex officio

Front jacket and page 6: Agnolo Bronzino, *Eleanora of Toledo
and Her Son*, c. 1545 (pl. 51, detail)

Back jacket: Israhel van Meckenem, *The Angry Wife*, from the
series *Scenes of Daily Life*, c. 1495/1503 (pl. 15)

Page 2: Simon Vouet, *The Toilette of Venus*, c. 1640–45
(pl. 26, detail)

Page 8: Fede Galizia, *Judith with the Head of Holofernes*, 1596
(pl. 32, detail)

Page 12: Lucas Cranach the Elder, *Judith*, c. 1530
(fig. 16, detail)

Contents

Sponsor's Statement

For centuries women have held positions of power and prestige as queens, spiritual leaders and rulers, and their representations in the visual arts have been as varied as their many roles. Ford Motor Company is proud to partner again with the University of Michigan Museum of Art to support *Women Who Ruled: Queens, Goddesses, Amazons 1500–1650* and offer audiences an opportunity to explore the fascinating histories of these extraordinary women.

The exhibition's rich presentation of images of female power offers us a unique vantage point from which to look at the role women leaders play in society today. In the twenty-first century, in business and in the legislature, in athletics, the arts, and the world of entertainment, women continue to navigate the complex paths of leadership and power, and public reactions to powerful women remain as varied and spirited as they were five centuries ago. *Women Who Ruled* reveals our kinship with our predecessors and also demonstrates the progress that has been made in modern times.

Women Who Ruled is part of a three-year series of exhibitions organized by the University of Michigan Museum of Art that Ford Motor Company is supporting. At Ford, we are committed to our national educational institutions and to the value and enjoyment of the arts. We believe that the arts play a vital role in our lives and our communities, and we are proud to expand our longstanding relationship with the University of Michigan. At Ford, we are committed to the arts and to the education and enjoyment that come from experiencing remarkable historical epics and works of genius. We are proud to build upon our longstanding partnership with the University through support for this exhibition and other visual and performing arts, community outreach, and educational programs.

We salute the University of Michigan Museum of Art and the other museums participating in this extraordinary exhibition.

Sandra E. Ulsh
PRESIDENT
FORD MOTOR COMPANY FUND

Director's Foreword

A few years ago, when I assumed the directorship of this museum, we recommitted ourselves to two concurrent and essential goals: mounting exhibitions that afforded (even mandated) the opportunity for the development and presentation of new scholarship and presenting this in lively and engaging ways for broad public audiences. Such goals have since been formalized within the museum's mission statement, reflecting our view of ourselves as an academic museum in a community setting—a duality that is not a conflict but an exceptional opportunity. Women Who Ruled reflects these simultaneous commitments as well as our larger belief that the visual arts can be part of the essential glue of civic life.

The bridge building between academic research and wide public consumption of fresh scholarly ideas can happen in a variety of ways, and many of these strategies are deployed in Women Who Ruled. The project seeks to bring fresh perspectives to historical material that has important—yet often overlooked or misunderstood—relevance to issues of our own time, namely the position of women in society, the wielding of power, and the complex responses we have to women and power. Women Who Ruled looks at a time in history that was extraordinary for the number of women who led European kingdoms, a time when a woman's right to rule became a central issue for many European societies and fed into an important debate about the "proper" place and role of women. It scarcely needs saying that such issues are at large in our own time, as women have come into increasing roles of influence in government, the military, business, sports, and the arts. By focusing on an earlier period in Western history when such issues absorbed public attention, we have hoped to bring greater understanding both to our own time and to a set of historical images that demands our attention.

This publication and exhibition are first and foremost about images and *their* power. Readers of this volume will discover how visual images in Renaissance and Baroque Europe were a key way in which the issue of female empowerment was described, conveyed to others, and sometimes contained. Both this publication and the exhibition which it accompanies seek to look at significant images from the European tradition afresh by examining them in something approaching their original historical context, by seeking to discover the power they held in their own time. The images range from depictions of woman rulers—iconic figures such as Queen Elizabeth I of Britain, Catherine de' Medici, and Marie de' Medici—to mythical, historical, and Biblical figures important in the period's visual culture. By extension, we invite readers and viewers to consider the role of images—specifically imagery of women—in our own media-saturated culture, as they relate to the representation, construction, and enactment of gender roles and styles.

It has felt particularly important to develop this project in the setting of a public university that has a long and sincere commitment to the education of the individual. Just as the University of Michigan has rededicated itself in recent times to the value of diversity, it was an early pioneer in coeducation, graduating its first women from a single, non-segregated campus in the nineteenth century. We recognize that the informed exploration of role and gender models, the presentation of our public figures, and concerns over female sexuality and beauty continue to be important subjects for our students of today, both male and female, at what is a critical period in their own lives. As historians, we believe there is much to be learned from the past and the images that previous cultures have left to us. This publication is part of a much larger investigation that will center on the Ann Arbor campus throughout the first half of 2002 in a multi-disciplinary theme semester entitled "Gender, Power, and Representation." It will include an array of courses, public lectures, performances, film screenings, and companion exhibitions. We are delighted that *Women Who Ruled* has served as the catalyst for this broader exploration of issues surrounding gender and its representation.

Work began on what has become *Women Who Ruled* in 1998, and has been led throughout by the museum's talented and exceptionally dedicated curator of Western art, Annette Dixon. I am truly pleased to present the fruits of Dr. Dixon's extensive research and her collaboration with academic partners at the University of Michigan and around the world. She is to be congratulated for bringing together such fascinating research strands, exemplary colleagues, and key loans during a period of less than four years when she has had many other exhibition and research commitments to contend with as well.

The many lenders to *Women Who Ruled* have been critical to the exhibition and this publication, although space precludes my naming them all here. Let me simply say that their generosity in sharing priceless works of art with us and our audiences inspires us at a time when many museums are being more guarded in allowing their objects to travel. Yet without this generosity, the power of engaging with original works of art through the exhibition format would be lost to all of us. Equally, the participation of the exhibition's touring venues has been vital to its success, and we are indebted to the staff at these fine institutions.

Clearly, a project involving a publication of this ambition and such a substantial number of loans and lending institutions has required the support of many. Both this exhibition and publication have been generously supported by the Ford Motor Company, without whose exceptional philanthropic leadership a project of this scope would not have been possible. My special thanks go to John Rintamaki, group vice president and chief of staff at Ford Motor Company (as well as a member of this museum's National Advisory Board). Thanks as well are due to Sandy Ulsh, vice president and executive director of the Ford Motor Company Fund; Cynthia Dodd, contributions programs manager, arts and culture; and Jim Graham, contributions program manager, education.

Additional essential support has come from many sources. The Samuel H. Kress Foundation has given generously through its "Old Masters in Context" program, while the National Endowment for the Arts made the first substantial grant to this project at a critical stage when it might otherwise have languished. Both are to be congratulated for sharing our vision of bringing complex issues in the visual arts to broad audiences. Our thanks also go to a donor who has chosen to remain anonymous, but whose leadership as a pioneering woman of strength and individuality is a model to all of us who know her and count her as a friend. The Friends of the Museum of Art have made a vital contribution, as have the following University of Michigan units: The Office of the Provost, the Institute for Research on Women and Gender, the Office of the Associate Provost for Academic Affairs, the Office of the Vice President for Research, the College of Literature, Science and the Arts, the Horace H. Rackham School of Graduate Studies, the Film and Video Studies Program, the Institute for the Humanities, the History of Art Department, the Center for the Education of Women, the Medieval and Early Modern Studies Program, the School of Music, and the Women's Studies Program. We trust that the results will be part of a continuing conversation between the images of the past and the issues of today, and that these results—not simply *Women Who Ruled* but the larger dialogue which we hope it elicits—are worthy of the confidence, faith, and commitment of so many.

James Christen Steward
DIRECTOR
THE UNIVERSITY OF MICHIGAN MUSEUM OF ART

Acknowledgments

Over the past few years as I have worked on this project, Renaissance and Baroque images of assertive women have proven fascinating to me for the ways in which they reveal patrons and artists grappling with how to represent women who broke traditional expectations for female behavior. As we live in an era when women are increasingly redefining gender boundaries and challenging the ways women are represented in today's media, we can look with interest at an earlier period when images of powerful women were being fashioned. I hope that viewers of the exhibition and readers of this volume will be stimulated to look at these Old Master images in a way they might not have done before. And I trust that they will look with a fresh eye at today's images of female power.

A loan exhibition of such scope as this one is the product of many who have helped it come to realization, both inside the organizing institution and outside of it. Among lenders to the exhibition, I owe a particular debt of gratitude to the following, who made special efforts to facilitate loans to the exhibition: Sue Reed at the Museum of Fine Arts, Boston; Marjorie Cohn at the Harvard University Art Museums, Fogg Art Museum, Cambridge; George Keyes at the Detroit Institute of Arts; Annamaria Petrioli Tofani at the Uffizi Gallery, Florence; Antony Griffiths, Andrew Burnett, and David Ward at the British Museum, London; George Goldner, Nadine Orenstein, and Gary Tinterow at the Metropolitan Museum of Art, New York; Michel Amandry, Laure Beaumont-Maillet, Sylviane Dailleau, and Hélène Fauré, at the Bibliothèque nationale de France, Paris; Louise Lippincott at the Carnegie Museum of Art, Pittsburgh; Betsy Rosasco and Maureen McCormick at the Art Museum, Princeton University; Mitchell Merling at the John and Mable Ringling Museum of Art, Sarasota; Jon Culverhouse at Burghley House, Stamford, Lincolnshire; Lawrence Nichols at the Toledo Art Museum; Alison Luchs at the National Gallery of Art, Washington; and Helena Wright at the National Museum of American History, Smithsonian Institution, Washington. Christopher Foley and the anonymous lender of a painting by Hendrick Goltzius went out of their way to enable the loan of their works to the exhibition. Peter Nahum kindly negotiated the loan of a work from a private collection.

For additional critical and intellectual support, the following museum and library colleagues played a critical role: Suzanne McClelland at the Art Institute of Chicago; Ellen Sharp at the Detroit Institute of Arts; Roberta Waddell at the New York Public Library;

Sylvie Merian and Kathleen Stuart at The Pierpont Morgan Library, New York; Serena Padovani at the Galleria Palatina, Palazzo Pitti, Florence; Caterina Caneva at the Uffizi Gallery, Florence; Raffaela Ausenda at the Castello Sforzesco, Milan; Rossella Vodret at the Galleria Nazionale d'Arte Antica, Palazzo Barberini, Rome; Sivigliano Alloisi at the Galleria Nazionale d'Arte Antica, Palazzo Corsini, Rome; Andrea de Marchi at the Galleria Doria Pamphili, Rome; Pierluigi Leone di Castris and Nicola Spinosa at the Museo e Gallerie Nazionali di Capodimonte, Naples; Plenia Arnoldi at the Galleria Sabauda, Turin; and Chiara Maida at the Galleria dell'Accademia, Venice.

I would like to acknowledge the scholars on the international advisory committee for this exhibition: Mieke Bal, Natalie Davis, Patricia Emison, Mary Rogers, Diane Russell, and Patricia Simons. I would like to thank other scholars who generously offered counsel: Svetlana Alpers, Sarah Cohen, Richard Falkiner, Creighton Gilbert, and Sir Roy Strong. Special thanks are owed to University of Michigan faculty who, early on, brought their expertise to bear on the project: Naomi André, Ward Bissell, Celeste Brusati, Stephen Campbell, Alina Clej, Glenda Dickerson, Jessica Fogel, Barbara Frederickson, Anne Herrmann, Diane Hughes, Ejner Jensen, Helmut Puff, Patricia Simons, Sidonie Smith, Domna Stanton, Abigail Stewart, Gaylyn Studlar, Valerie Traub, Thomas Willette, and Ralph Williams. The enthusiasm of these faculty members led to the co-organization of the theme semester "Gender, Power, and Representation" by the Women's Studies Program and the Museum of Art. I am enormously grateful to past director of Women's Studies, Sidonie Smith, and current director, Pamela Reid, for their tremendous enthusiasm and leadership. Donna Ainsworth and Maureen McDonnell contributed greatly to the administration of the theme semester.

I am grateful to the essayists in this volume—Merry Wiesner-Hanks, Mieke Bal, and Bettina Baumgärtel—for their willingness to engage with the issues raised by the works in this exhibition with vigor and insight. I owe a particular debt of gratitude to Karein Goertz, who translated Bettina Baumgärtel's essay. To my colleagues at Merrell Publishers, I offer my heartfelt thanks for shepherding the manuscript through the various phases of its production with utmost patience and understanding: Hugh Merrell, Julian Honer, and Matt Hervey.

I would also like to acknowledge those at the University of Michigan Museum of Art whose hard work and dedication have made the project possible. I owe an enormous debt of gratitude to James Steward, Director of the University of Michigan Museum of Art, who reacted with enormous enthusiasm to a little kernel of an idea, which over the course of more than three years he consistently nurtured. His faith and encouragement were of inestimable importance to the project. I would also like to thank the following: for adminstrative oversight of the exhibition at many crucial stages, Kathryn Huss; for reading this manuscript in its various stages and offering most welcome counsel as to it presentation, Karen Goldbaum, Carole McNamara, and Ruth Slavin; for graphic design in the exhibition and programs, Steven Hixson; for photography, Patrick Young and Sophie Rasul; for registrarial assistance, Lori Mott and Ann Sinfield; for computer expertise, Antonia Kramer and Brian Cors; for preparation and installation, Kevin Canze, Katie Carew, Kirsten Neelands, and Brendnt Rae; for admininstrative assistance, Jo Lau and Stacie Williams; for guidance with the budget, Terri Gable; for development, Tena Achen,

Courtney Whitehead, and Karen Prosser; for publicity and public relations, Karen Meske; for education programs and special events, Ruth Slavin, Pamela Reister, and Deborah Swartz; for Museum shop sales and ticketing, Suzanne Witthoff; and for security, Billie Bahr, Wayne Kilbourn, Thomas Walsh, Xu Yong, and Stanley Zulch. Katherine Weiss and Karen Wight contributed energetic and meticulous work on logistical aspects of the project. I am grateful to Karen Goldbaum for her help shaping the manuscript and to Carol Stein for editorial assistance.

This exhibition would not have been possible without the help of research assistants, to whom I am grateful for their countless hours of toil and their inspired observations. These include Emily Baumgartner; Anne Duroe; Florence Friedrich, who devoted tremendous energy to the project for a year and a half; Carmen Higgenbotham; and Sandra Seekins. Without their tireless work this project would have been much diminished.

Annette Dixon
CURATOR OF WESTERN ART
THE UNIVERSITY OF MICHIGAN MUSEUM OF ART

Lenders to the Exhibition

Albion, Michigan, Albion College

Angers, France, Musées d'Angers

Ann Arbor, Michigan, University of Michigan Museum of Art

Austin, Texas, Harry Ransom Humanities Research Center,
      The University of Texas at Austin

Baltimore, Maryland, The Walters Art Museum

Berkeley, California, University of California, Berkeley Art Museum

Boston, Massachusetts, Museum of Fine Arts, Boston

Brussels, Belgium, Royal Library of Belgium, Coins and Medals

Cambridge, Massachusetts, Fogg Art Museum, Harvard University Art Museums

Cambridge, Massachusetts, Harvard University, Houghton Library

Chapel Hill, North Carolina, Ackland Art Museum,
      The University of North Carolina at Chapel Hill

Chicago, Illinois, Art Institute of Chicago

Cincinnati, Ohio, Cincinnati Art Museum

Cleveland, Ohio, Cleveland Museum of Art

Columbia, Missouri, Museum of Art and Archaeology,
      University of Missouri-Columbia

Christopher Foley

Detroit, Michigan, The Detroit Institute of Arts

Düsseldorf, Germany, Kunstmuseum Düsseldorf

Flint, Michigan, Flint Institute of Arts

Florence, Italy, Uffizi Gallery

London, England, The British Museum

London, England, Victoria and Albert Museum

Los Angeles, California, Los Angeles County Museum of Art

Minneapolis, Minnesota, The Minneapolis Institute of Arts

New Haven, Connecticut, The Beinecke Rare Book and Manuscript Library,
      Yale University

New York, New York, The Metropolitan Museum of Art

New York, New York, The New York Public Library

Omaha, Nebraska, Joslyn Art Museum
Ottawa, Canada, National Gallery of Canada, Ottawa
Paris, France, Bibliothèque nationale de France
Paris, France, Musée du Louvre
Peter Nahum (private collection)
Pittsburgh, Pennsylvania, Carnegie Museum of Art
Princeton, New Jersey, The Art Museum, Princeton University
Providence, Rhode Island, The Museum of Art, Rhode Island School of Design
Raleigh, North Carolina, North Carolina Museum of Art
Saint Bonaventure, New York, Saint Bonaventure University, Friedsam Memorial
    Library, Franciscan Institute Collection
San Francisco, California, Fine Arts Museums of San Francisco, Achenbach Foundation
    for Graphic Arts
Santa Barbara, California, University of California, Santa Barbara,
    University Art Museum
Sarasota, Florida, The John and Mable Ringling Museum of Art
Stamford, Lincolnshire, England, The Burghley House Collection
Toledo, Ohio, Toledo Museum of Art
Washington, D.C., National Gallery of Art
Washington, D.C., Smithsonian Institution National Museum of American History,
    Behring Center
Anonymous private collector

Introduction

ANNETTE DIXON

Unprecedented numbers of women ruled states and kingdoms during the period 1500 to 1650, and the presence of so many female rulers prompted a burgeoning of images of powerful women. While it was rare for a woman to rule in her own right—as was the case with Elizabeth I and Christina of Sweden—accidents of history thrust a few into positions of power as queens, queen regents of great kingdoms, or heads of minor states. Notable among these are Isabella of Castile, who ruled Castile and Aragon jointly with her husband Ferdinand; Mary Tudor and Elizabeth I in England; Mary Stuart in Scotland; France's Catherine de' Medici, Marie de' Medici, and Anne of Austria; and Christina of Sweden.[1] Visual images were a key way in which women rulers affirmed their right to rule and negotiated their positions in courtly culture and even in international diplomatic circles.

There were, of course, powerful female rulers before and after this period (one thinks of Eleanor of Aquitaine in the twelfth century, Blanche of Castile (pl. 1) in France in the thirteenth century, or Catherine the Great in Russia in the eighteenth century), but the late sixteenth century saw no fewer than three female heads of European principalities ruling at the same time: Elizabeth I, Mary Stuart, and Catherine de' Medici. This introduced a new concern into the traditional anxiety about appropriate female roles—the capacity of women to govern. The issue of female agency became a burning one and emerged also as a key theme in the art of the time. Ruling women, in concert with court advisers and artists, developed strategies for representing themselves as able, appropriate, and properly sanctioned leaders, much as male heads of state had long done. At the same time, the rise of printmaking during this period provided a new vehicle for those outside court circles to engage in arguments about women and power in word and image. Visual imagery arose to accommodate a range of opinions about female power—from approval, to disapproval, to ambivalence.

These 150 years coincided with the development of the early modern nation-state and its consolidation of political power not only through wars and forays into imperialism, but also through international marriage alliances. Marriage, and therefore women, took on a new significance since marrying a rich, foreign, highborn woman could both increase a state's coffers and secure a dynastic line, as was the case with Eleanora of Toledo and Cosimo I de' Medici, Catherine de' Medici and Henri II, Marie de' Medici and Henri IV,

Opposite: Hendrick Goltzius, *Helen of Troy,* 1615 (pl. 25, detail)

and Anne of Austria and Louis XIII. Through her advisers, Elizabeth I engaged in marriage negotiations in order to form international alliances, but, seeing that marriage would put her under the domination of a husband, she thwarted those negotiations.

In the context of nation building, the state portrait emerges as a tool of propaganda and prestige. It was appropriated in interesting ways by female rulers, forced to devise their own symbols of rulership, adopting alter-egos from myth, literature, the Bible, and history in order to fashion self-images that projected power, identity, authority, and an image for their dynasty. Other women making incursions into the public arena, such as noblewomen protecting their lands during the many wars that marked this period, fashioned themselves as Amazons or warriors drawing upon the stories of earlier valiant women such as Joan of Arc. Facilitating the new overlay of imagery employed by these rulers and noblewomen, printmaking technology made it easier to disseminate these portraits and was an important factor in introducing imagery of powerful women into the popular visual culture of the time.

As we cast our eyes over this broad spectrum of imagery, certain patterns of representation recur, corresponding with traditional roles and characterizations of women in myth and in society, but often interpreting them in new and complex ways. This exhibition looks at a selection of nearly one hundred images of powerful female figures created during this period in a great variety of media: paintings, drawings, prints, book illustrations, sculpture, and the decorative arts. Examining their historical contexts, the exhibition aims, wherever possible, to discern the complex range of reactions to female power that were both reflected in and inspired by these images. How would men and women have responded to this imagery, and how did such image-making affect the social and political landscape? The essayists in this volume draw from their own rich stores of scholarship and experience to provide additional insight into these topics.

We have organized the works in the exhibition thematically to highlight the consistently compelling ways that women in power were depicted; these also correspond with familiar, traditional—even stereotypical—representations of women. The categories of wife, mother, and virgin, for example, constitute a traditionally accepted and socially sanctioned spectrum of female existence in a male-dominated society. Within these states or roles, however, women found ways to cultivate power, and to communicate the benefits to society of carrying out these roles in an exemplary manner. On the other hand, sexually assertive women, who stepped out of those traditional, subjugated roles, sometimes becoming involved in seduction and murder of men for political gain, were perceived as threatening to the social order. The frequency of such representations of Biblical or mythological figures suggests the deep cultural ambivalence brought on by the sight of so many women in power.

It was important for a woman ruler and her supporters to justify her movement outside the typical areas of perceived female authority. One method was to link her with extraordinary, even divine qualities (pl. 2), or to depict her succeeding in male pursuits—as a warrior (pl. 3), for example. There are fascinating examples of such heroic associations, which are all the more remarkable for their ability to undercut hundreds of years of doctrine and popular culture suggesting that women's actions outside a circumscribed sphere represented a perversion of nature.

Opposite: By or after George Gower, *Portrait of Queen Elizabeth I, c. 1588* (pl. 63, detail)

In the pages that follow, essayists from different disciplines develop some of the lines of inquiry introduced above, offering diverse perspectives from which to understand images of female power during this period. Shedding new light on ways in which people of this period understood depictions of powerful women, they show that representations of strong women were exciting and vital to their cultures. In doing so, they bring these images alive for us today, revealing the ways in which such images played a role in an active controversy during this time about the scope and arena of women's power—whether women should have power, and where they should exercise it. Merry Wiesner-Hanks, Professor of History and Chair, University of Wisconsin–Milwaukee, discusses the simultaneous acceptance and questioning of women's authority in the state and household—two arenas for female power, seen through the lens of primary sources of the time. Mieke Bal, Professor of Theory of Literature, University of Amsterdam, examines the power struggle between the sexes played out in figurations of power, and reminds us of the impact that some of the images in this exhibition might have had on people in their daily lives during the Renaissance and Baroque periods. Bettina Baumgärtel, Chief Curator of the Department of Paintings, Kunstmuseum Düsseldorf, analyzes propagandistic images of rulers as gods or goddesses in which gender boundaries are respected or subverted, noting the utility of myth-making in consolidating state power.

These essays make it abundantly clear that, then and now, women in the public sphere carried with them the burden of their connection with the private sphere. While lines between the two spheres were often interrelated for women, they were never so for men, for whom ruling and acting publicly were separate from domestic life. By contrast, the question of female leadership was always connected with the issue of woman's traditional role. Female leaders were threatening because they upset, at a state level, the established male-female power balance in society, unleashing angst about uppity wives, dangerous seductresses, and female warriors gaining the upper hand in the domestic sphere. Whether they conveyed anxiety, ambivalence, or approval, images of powerful women were a crucial part of the arguments about women's changing social roles in this period.

NOTES

1 Isabella of Castile (1451–1504, reigned 1479–1504), Mary Tudor (1516–1558, reigned 1553–1558), Elizabeth I (1533–1603, reigned 1558–1603), Mary Stuart (1542–1587, reigned 1542–1567), Catherine de' Medici (1519–1589, regent 1560–1574), Marie de' Medici (1573–1642, regent 1610–1614), Anne of Austria (1601–1666, regent 1643–1651), and Christina of Sweden (1626–1689, reigned 1644–1654).

1

GRÉGOIRE HURET
French, 1606–1670
Blanche of Castile as
Minerva, title page in
Charles Combault
d'Auteuil, Blanche
infante de Castille,
mère de S. Louis...,
Paris, Antoine de
Sommaville, 1644

Engraving
220 × 160 mm (8⅝ × 6¼ in.)
Cambridge, Harvard University,
Houghton Library

Combault d'Auteuil's treatise on
the life of Blanche of Castile was
published during the regency of
Anne of Austria. As the title page
for the work, Huret's engraving
of Blanche of Castile as Minerva
seems in itself to be an argument
in favor of women's capacity to
rule. Blanche of Castile, who
ruled France as regent during the
thirteenth century, was one of
the historic queens who was held
up during the seventeenth
century as a model for
contemporary women rulers.

BLANCHE INFANTE DE CASTILLE.

Os suum aperuit sapientiæ; et lex clementiæ in lingua eius. Prouerb.3². jnMuliere forti.

PER TAL VARIAR SON QVI

Lo here her *Type*, who was of late, the Proppe of *Belgia*; Stay of *France*:
Spaines Foyle Faiths Shield; and Queene of STATE; Of Armes, and Learning; FATE, and Chance
In briefe; of women, nere was scene, so greate a Prince; so good a Queene.

Fr. De. Sculptor.   ELIZABETHA REGINA.   Nic: Hillyard delin : et excud : cum priuilegio Maiest :

Jo: Dauies

Are to be Sould at the Angell in Lumbard
Streete By Roger Daniell

2
FRANCIS DELARAM
English, c. 1590–1627
After NICHOLAS
HILLIARD
English, c. 1547–1619
**Portrait of Queen
Elizabeth I**

c. 1617
Engraving
317 × 221 mm (12½ × 8¾ in.)
London, The British Museum,
Department of Prints and Drawings

Delaram's print is based on a
drawing by Nicholas Hilliard,
which no longer exists. Elizabeth
is shown as the Virgin Mary and
as the Woman of the Apocalypse,
based on imagery from the Book
of Revelation. Such imagery was
not used in Elizabeth's lifetime,
but fits well with disaffection
with Stuart rule, when Protestants
looked back to her as a heroine
of their cause.

3
THOMAS CECIL
English, active c. 1625–1640
**Truth Presents the Queen
with a Lance**

c. 1625
Engraving
273 × 299 mm (10¾ × 11¾ in.)
London, The British Museum,
Department of Prints and Drawings

This posthumous engraving
shows Elizabeth I as an Amazon
in armor and on horseback,
while the Armada is defeated in
the background. Her horse
tramples the Beast of the
Apocalypse, symbolizing Roman
Catholicism. A woman
surrounded by flames appears at
the mouth of a cave, offering a
lance to the queen. Holding a
book inscribed *Truth*, she
symbolizes the truth of
Protestantism.

ELIZABETHA ANGLIÆ ET HIBERNIÆ REGINÆ. &c.

Sould by Peter Stent

T: Cecill sculp

Women's Authority in the State and Household in Early Modern Europe

MERRY WIESNER-HANKS

Women who held and used power were clearly viewed as threatening in Western culture since its beginning. The *Enuma Elish*, the creation account of the ancient Babylonians, tells the story of Tiamat, the goddess who battled her grandson Marduk for primacy; Marduk killed Tiamat, "cast down her carcass ... split her skull ... cut the arteries of her blood ... split her open like a mussel into two parts," with which he created the earth and the sky.[1] In the more familiar creation account told in Genesis, Eve's desire "to be like divine beings who know good and bad" led her to disobey Yahweh's commandment, for which he condemned her to painful childbirth and subjection to her husband's authority: "he shall rule over you" (Gen. 3.5.16). In Greek mythology, every hero from Achilles to Heracles fought the Amazons, that legendary group of female warriors who lived at the boundaries of civilization, and Theseus's final defeat of the Amazons was crucial to his role as the originator of Athenian democracy (pls. 4, 5). All of these stories were part of oral traditions that later came to be written down, and were also portrayed in visual images for public display and private use. Babylonian midwives, for example, were ordered to recount the story of Marduk's creation of the world out of Tiamat's split body to women when they were in labor, and the Amazons were portrayed on ceramic knee guards worn by Athenian women when they carded wool. Eve became a common figure in Christian visual and verbal imagery, portrayed sometimes as the sole cause of human separation from God and always as the cause for women's inferior status (pl. 7).

Examples of women wielding power for the benefit of society were less common, though not unknown. Hebrew Scripture tells the story of Deborah, a prophet who informed the general Barak that he should lead an army against the Canaanite general Sisera and then accompanied his army (pl. 8). With Deborah's encouragement, Barak's forces were successful, and Sisera himself was killed by another powerful woman, Jael. Both of these women are praised in the book of Judges, with Deborah described as a "mother of Israel," and Jael as "most blessed of women." Biblical apocrypha included the story of Judith, the beautiful widow from the small town of Bethulia, who cut off the head of the Assyrian general Holofernes after convincing him to take her into his tent and getting him drunk (pl. 11). Greek mythology contributed the figure of Athena (Minerva in the Roman pantheon), generally portrayed in breastplate and helmet (pl. 12).

Opposite: Paris Bordone,
Athena Scorning the Advances of Hephaestus,
c. 1555–60 (pl. 12, detail)

From ancient history came the stories of Zenobia, the queen of Palmyra in Syria, who led her troops against the Romans (pl. 13), and Lucretia, whose rape by the tyrant Sextus Tarquinius led to her suicide, and eventually to the killing of Tarquinius and the establishment of the Roman Republic by her husband and father (pl. 17).[2]

These ancient and Biblical examples continued to be discussed and portrayed throughout the Middle Ages in Europe, but they came to have particular resonance in the period of the late Renaissance for a variety of reasons. Renaissance humanists were fascinated with the classical past, and searched ancient history and mythology for models to emulate and avoid. Christian humanists and later Protestant and Catholic reformers put greater emphasis on the Bible as the center of Christian teachings, using the stories in both the Old and New Testaments as the basis for their sermons in the vernacular and for learned treatises in Latin.

Along with this fascination with classical and biblical texts, political and social developments contributed to concerns about women's power. Because of a series of dynastic accidents, women ruled as queens in their own right or as regents at some point during the sixteenth and seventeenth centuries in almost all of the major nations of western Europe and many of the smaller states in Italy and Germany. Protestant and Catholic notions of the ideal household viewed the husband as its clear head, but gave the wife authority over her children and servants, and in some instances even dubbed her "coruler" (fig. 1). Most women spent some of their lives as widows, a status in which they had a great degree of legal and economic independence. In all three of these cases—rulers, wives, and widows—women had not only power, but also authority, that is, power that was supported by legal, political, and religious institutions and by cultural norms. Visual images of female power produced during this period, even those of mythological or biblical figures, must be read within this context of women's socially sanctioned authority. This essay will explore the two arenas of that authority of most concern to early modern Europeans: the state and the household. In both of these arenas, dynastic traditions, religious doctrine, and demographic realities gave women authority as well as power, but this was disturbing to many commentators and gave rise to extended intellectual debates and various attempts to limit that authority through laws and their enforcement.

In examining the historical setting in which artistic images were produced, it is important not to differentiate too sharply between "image" and "reality." One of the central insights of interdisciplinary cultural scholarship over the last several decades has been the continual interaction between these two, the ways in which literary and artistic "texts" and historical "context" blend and interweave. Real people shaped the way that they were portrayed (both textually and visually), and also shaped their own actual outward appearance and personality in a process that has come to be called "self-fashioning."[3] Early modern Europeans fashioned themselves on ideals that they read about, heard about, or saw, so that the images came to shape the way people looked and behaved. This process was not new in this period—altering one's behavior or persona in order to emulate a model had been part of Western education since the classical period— but it was made more explicit. Manuals such as Castiglione's The Courtier (1528) advised men and women how to behave in various situations, suggesting that proper clothing

Fig. 1 Attributed to Paulus Moreelse, *Portrait of a family saying grace before a meal, with a servant stoking the fire and a landscape seen through an open door*, 1602, oil on panel, 76.2 × 104.1 cm (30 × 41 in.), Christie's Images Inc.

and deportment could be an avenue to influence.[4] Some thinkers worried about this process, viewing it as promoting artificiality, shallowness, and hypocrisy, while others supported it, arguing that it encouraged civility and good manners. Both sides in this debate frequently invoked women; those who attacked self-fashioning argued that it made men more like women—vain, frivolous, concerned with their appearance—while those who supported it noted that dependence on someone more powerful was a reality of life, and that smart courtiers, like smart wives, should recognize this.[5]

The debate about self-fashioning and the discussion of female power were part of a larger intellectual debate about the nature and proper role of women that took place in many countries of Europe during the fifteenth through the seventeenth centuries. This debate often goes by its French title, the *Querelle des femmes*, and it involved many male and female writers, including both prominent literary figures and hack authors.[6] Pro-women writers such as Christine de Pizan, Cornelius Agrippa of Nettesheim, Rachel Speght, Moderata Fonte, and Lucrezia Marinella generally provided long lists of illustrious and virtuous women—including the Biblical and classical figures discussed above—to argue that women were capable of great deeds and moral virtue.[7] Misogynist writers such as Jean Bodin and Joseph Swetnam provided long lists of deceitful and dangerous women, arguing that both nature and God had ordained women's inferiority.[8] A few writers argued both sides of the issue, particularly in simple works written in the vernacular.[9] Such works were clearly written with an eye to the market rather than from deep conviction, which has led some recent analysts to view the whole debate about women as simply a literary exercise, though most scholars judge it to have been a matter of serious cultural debate.[10]

The debate about women also found visual expression in the early modern period. Treatises profiling heroic and virtuous women were often illustrated (pls. 9, 10, 14), and single-sheet prints that were hung in taverns or people's homes often showed female virtues and vices, with the virtuous women depicted as those of the classical or biblical past, and the vice-ridden dressed in contemporary clothes. The favorite metaphor for the virtuous wife was either the snail or the tortoise, both animals that never leave their "houses" and are totally silent, although such images were never as widespread as those depicting wives beating their husbands or hiding their lovers from them (pl. 15 and fig. 2). Most of the prints, which people purchased to hang on their walls or were published as part of emblem books, portrayed the same negative stereotypes of women as the written attacks; women are shown with their hands in men's purses, tempting men by displaying naked breasts, or neglecting their housework. Artists frequently portrayed misogynist stories involving classical or biblical figures—such as Socrates' wife, Xanthippe, nagging him, or Aristotle being so seduced by the beauty of Phyllis that he allowed her to ride him around a garden, or Delilah tempting Samson—so that these became part of popular culture as well as that of Europe's learned elite (pls. 6, 16).[11] Judging by what has survived, these negative images appear to have been more popular than positive ones, which is also true of literary works; learned attacks, satirical critiques, and misogynist stories generally were republished more often than works that praised women.[12]

Fig. 2 Anonymous, *Battle over the Pants*, woodcut frontispiece to the play *The Evil Smoke* by Hans Sachs, published by Georg Merckel in Nuremberg, c. 1553, 73 × 64 mm (2⅞ × 2½ in.), Museen der Stadt Nürnberg

WOMEN'S AUTHORITY IN THE STATE

Beginning in the sixteenth century, the debate about women also became one about female rulers, sparked primarily by dynastic accidents in many countries that led to women serving as advisers to child kings or ruling in their own right—Isabella in Castile, Mary and Elizabeth Tudor in England, Mary Stuart in Scotland, Catherine de' Medici and Anne of Austria in France. Both as rulers and as regents, women held politically sanctioned authority, not simply operating as "the power behind the throne," but their ability to do so was often challenged. The questions vigorously and at times viciously disputed directly concerned what we would term the social construction of gender: could a woman's being born into a royal family and educated to rule allow her to overcome the limitations of her sex? Should it? Or stated another way: which was (or should be) the stronger determinant of character and social role, gender or rank?

The most extreme opponents of female rule were Protestants who went into exile on the continent during the reign of Mary Tudor, including Anthony Gilby, Thomas Becon, Christopher Goodman, and John Knox. They compared Mary with Jezebel, arguing that female rule was unnatural, unlawful, and contrary to Scripture. Knox titled his treatise *The First Blast of the Trumpet Against the Monstrous Regiment of Women* (1558), directing it against Mary Stuart as well as Mary Tudor and asserting that both nature and Scripture placed all women under male authority, "excepting none." Knox wrote: "A woman promoted to sit in the seat of God, that is, to teach, to judge or to reign above man, is a monster in nature, contumely to God, and a thing most repugnant to his will and ordinance" (fol. 16r.). The word "monster" was used to describe female rulers by other authors as well, echoing Aristotle's notion that the female sex in general is monstrous. Thus, for these authors, being female was a condition that could never be overcome, and subjects of female rulers needed no other justification for rebelling than their monarch's sex, for queens regnant were unnatural and could never have true authority. This suspicion of female rulers may have been influenced by the recent experiences of the German and Swiss cities in which they were exiled, against which noblewomen such as the Duchesses Bianca Maria Sforza of Milan or Elisabeth of Bavaria-Landshut led military actions.

Gilby, Goodman, and Knox all had the misfortune to publish their works in 1558, the very year that Mary Tudor died and Elizabeth I assumed the throne, making their position as both Protestants and opponents of female rule rather tricky. A number of courtiers realized that defenses of female rule would be likely to help them win favor in Elizabeth's eyes, and they advanced arguments against viewing a woman's sex as an absolute block to rulership. Thomas Smith in *De Republica Anglorum: The maner of Governement or Policie of the Realme of England* (1583) stated bluntly that "an absolute Queene, and absolute Dutches or Countesse" had a clear right to rule, and John Aylmer, in a *Harborowe for Faithfull and Trewe Subjectes* (1559), disputed both the Scriptural and natural law arguments against female authority. Aylmer argued that Scriptural prohibitions of women teaching or speaking were only relevant for the particular groups to which they were addressed, and that a woman's sex did not automatically exclude her from rule just as a boy king's age or a handicapped king's infirmity did not exclude him. He asserted that even a married queen could rule legitimately, for she could be subject to her husband in her private life, yet monarch to him and all other men in her public—a concept of split identity that Aylmer and other political theorists described as the ruler's "two bodies" and what we might describe as a distinction between the queenship and the queen. (For a more extensive discussion of this issue, see the essay in this volume by Bettina Baumgärtel.) A queen might thus be clearly female in her body and sexuality, but still exhibit the masculine qualities regarded as necessary in a ruler because of traits she had inherited or learned. Aylmer and other defenders of female rule were thus clearly separating sex from gender, and even approaching an idea of androgyny as a desirable state for the public persona of female monarchs.

It is perhaps not very surprising that Aylmer and his associates were writing during the rule of Elizabeth, the early modern monarch who most astutely used both feminine and masculine gender stereotypes to her own advantage. Elizabeth often chose to wear clothing that emphasized her breasts, hips, and narrow shoulders (pl. 18); carried objects associated with women such as fans (pl. 63); and, as she grew older, dressed in white, a symbol of purity and virginity. At the same time, she spoke excellent Latin when the situation warranted it, occasionally wore a small armor breastplate, and approved of portraits showing her with symbols of authority, such as a scepter (pls. 19, 20). Henry VIII's disappointment at Elizabeth's birth—he had her mother, Anne Boleyn, executed so he could try for a son with yet another wife—did not prevent her from attaining a fine Renaissance education, and she learned to speak and write well in several languages. The death of her younger brother, Edward VI, and older sister, Mary I, made Elizabeth queen at age twenty-five, for, despite doubts about women's rational capacities and ruling capabilities, and all of Knox's harsh words, sixteenth-century Europeans were reluctant to upset established rules of succession; blood could still overcome some of the limitations of gender, at least for rulers.

Elizabeth used her unusual status as a virgin queen (immortalized in "Virginia," the name given originally by the English to all of North America not held by the Spanish or French) and as a person who combined masculine and feminine qualities skillfully in both her actions and words, noting in a speech apparently given to her troops at Tilbury camp after the defeat of the Spanish Armada: "I know I have the body but of a weak and feeble woman, but I have the heart and stomach of a king—and of a king of England too ... rather than any dishonor shall grow by me, I myself will take up arms, I myself will be your general, judge, and rewarder of every one of your virtues in the field."[13] She was an extremely effective ruler, preferring diplomacy to war, building up the national treasury, supporting the navy and commerce, and encouraging the establishment of colonies and the disruption of Spanish trade with the New World. Most historians view her reign as one in which England first became a major world power, creating the basis for the later establishment of the British Empire. Though Elizabeth clearly recognized that her situation would have been very different had she been born a boy, she did nothing to change gender structures in England or to lessen the legal disabilities facing women. In this she follows the pattern of most queens throughout the world, who viewed their status as monarchs—in Elizabeth's words as "we Princes ... set on stages in the sight and view of all of world"—as overriding their status as women.[14]

Elizabeth clearly realized that people expected monarchs to be male, and that qualities judged masculine by her peers—physical bravery, stamina, wisdom, duty—should be emphasized whenever a monarch chose to appear or speak in public. This can also be seen in other female rulers, such as Catherine and Marie de' Medici, who both served as regents during the minorities of their sons.[15] (Catherine, the wife of Henri II of France, was also a very influential queen mother for nearly forty years during the reigns of her largely ineffectual male offspring.) Catherine planned and choreographed extravagant festivals and performances featuring her children and courtiers designed to impress visiting ambassadors; these were later depicted in the Valois Tapestries, now at the Uffizi Gallery in Florence, with herself and her family members prominently displayed in dignified and heroic poses (fig. 3 and pl. 21). Her younger relative Marie de' Medici, wife of Henri IV of France, had first observed the role of symbolism in the ceremonies surrounding her proxy marriage to Henri IV, which included musical productions, plays,

Fig. 3 Antoine Caron, French, c. 1521–c. 1599, *Excursion to the Island in the Adour*, 1565, black chalk, brown and black ink, gray-brown wash, heightened with white, 348 × 492 mm (13¾ × 19⅜ in.), New York, The Pierpont Morgan Library, Purchase as the gift of the Fellows, 1955

paintings, and nearly life-size sugar statues of herself and her husband-to-be. After the assassination of her husband, Marie sponsored a large number of architectural and artistic projects, including paintings, medals, and palaces, in which she had both her husband and herself portrayed as mythological characters or in complex allegories based on events in their lives, fashioning a self linked to goddesses and abstract virtues. The most dramatic of these, Peter Paul Rubens's cycle of twenty-four enormous paintings illustrating Marie's own life commissioned by the queen for her new (and equally enormous) Luxembourg palace, shows Marie in one canvas with the attributes of male rulers, including a scepter and the scales of justice, and of male warriors, including a helmet and cannon. (These images were frequently copied on a smaller scale by later artists [see pls. 22, 23].)

The more successful male rulers in early modern Europe also tried to connect themselves whenever possible with qualities and objects judged male. They appeared or had themselves depicted on horseback wearing armor and carrying weapons, commissioned portraits including all their progeny, and gave speeches or supported court plays highlighting their wisdom and reason. Sometimes this linkage had ironic results, however. Jeffrey Merrick has demonstrated, for example, that French monarchs and their supporters used the image of a beehive under a "king bee" as a model of harmony under royal rule and a community whose existence depended on the health of its monarch; even scientists spoke of the beehive in this way, for they regarded nature as the best source of examples for appropriate political structures, which they then termed "natural."[16] When the invention of the microscope made it clear the king bee was a queen, both royal propagandists and scientists tried to downplay her sex as long as possible, embarrassed that nature would provide such a demonstration of "unnatural" female authority. (By the eighteenth century the sex of the queen bee was no longer ignored, but her role was now described as totally maternal, a symbol of motherhood rather than monarchy.)

A concern with masculinity, and particularly with demonstrating the autonomy expected of a man, pervades the political writings of Machiavelli, who used "effeminate" to describe the worst kind of ruler. "Effeminate" in the sixteenth century carried slightly different connotations than it does today, however, for strong heterosexual passion was not a sign of manliness, but could make one "effeminate," i.e., dominated by as well as similar to a woman. English commentators, for example, described Irish men as effeminate and inferior because they let both their wives and their sexual desires influence their actions. Strong same-sex attachments, on the other hand, were often regarded as a sign of virility, as long as they were accompanied by actions judged honorably masculine, such as effective military leadership, and not accompanied by actions judged feminine, such as emotional outbursts. Manliness, the best quality in either ruler or government, was demonstrated by the ability to use reason to take advantage of every situation; as Machiavelli commented in The Prince (written 1513; published 1532): "Fortune is a woman, and if you want to keep her under, you've got to knock her around some."[17] No woman is mentioned by name in The Prince, an omission that becomes quite noticeable when Machiavelli discusses Ferdinand at length without mentioning Isabella; he does mention (by title only) Caterina Sforza, the Duchess of Forlì, but only to comment that she was one of the few rulers who had been helped by strong fortresses.

While Machiavelli used effectiveness as the only way to judge rulers or political structures and argued that authority should be based on power rather than the other way around (a position for which he was roundly condemned), Jean Bodin, the French jurist and political theorist, returned to Scripture and natural law in The Six Books of the Republic (1576), using these to oppose female rule. Bodin also stressed what would become in the seventeenth century the most frequently cited reason against it: that the state was like a household, and just as in a household the husband/father has authority and power over all others, so in the state a male monarch should always rule. Robert Filmer carried this even further in Patriarcha (written 1640s; published 1680), asserting that rulers derived all legal authority from the divinely sanctioned fatherly power of Adam, just as did all fathers. Male monarchs used husbandly and paternal imagery to justify their assertion of power over their subjects, as in James I's statements to parliament: "I am the Husband, and the whole Isle is my lawfull Wife .... By the law of nature the king becomes a natural father to all his lieges at his coronation .... A King is trewly Parens patriae, the politique father of his people."[18] Criticism of monarchs was also couched in paternal language; pamphlets directed against the crown during the revolt known as the Fronde in seventeenth-century France, for example, justified their opposition by asserting that the king was not properly fulfilling his fatherly duties.[19]

The link between royal and paternal authority could also work in the opposite direction to enhance the power of male heads of household. Just as subjects were deemed to have no or only a very limited right of rebellion against their ruler, so women and children were not to dispute the authority of the husband/father because both kings and fathers were held to have received their authority from God. The household was not viewed as private, but as the smallest political unit and so part of the public realm. Jean Bodin put it succinctly: "So we will leave moral discourse to the philosophers and theologians, and we will take up what is relative to political life, and speak of the husband's power over the wife, which is the source and origin of every human society.[20] Elizabeth I clearly recognized the power of this idea, for though she had many suitors, she never married, recognizing that if she did she would put herself in a very awkward position in a society that regarded husbandly and fatherly authority in the household as a model for good government in the larger political realm.[21]

Many analysts see the Protestant Reformation and, in England, Puritanism as further strengthening this paternal authority by granting male heads of household a much larger religious and supervisory role than they had under Catholicism.[22] The fact that Protestant clergy were themselves generally married heads of household also meant that ideas about clerical authority reinforced notions of paternal and husbandly authority; priests were now husbands, and husbands priests. Most Protestant writers also gave mothers a role in the religious and moral life of the household, but this was always secondary to that of fathers.

Protestant women such as Argula von Grumbach (c. 1490–c. 1564) in Germany or Elinor James (fl. 1680s) in England occasionally linked authority within the family to authority in the larger community for women as well as men. They argued that because the household was widely regarded as part of the public realm, women already had public duties; therefore their speaking out on political or religious matters was simply an extension of their public role as mothers and wives.[23] This line of argument was generally rejected in the early modern period, and when nineteenth-century women's rights advocates again spoke of their duties as wives and mothers, the terms of the debate had shifted. By this time the household was regarded as part of the private sphere rather than the public, and women could not speak of political responsibilities as something they were already doing in the way that Grumbach or James had. Instead they argued that only by gaining political rights would women truly be able to carry out their private familial duties, because the political realm shaped family life so intensely in matters such as temperence, education, and health. These "domestic" or "relational" feminists, as they are termed, thus acknowledged the private nature of the household, though one wonders if in the long run a continued assertion of the public nature of women's domestic responsibilites might have proved a more secure base for the expansion of women's political rights.[24]

Links between the realm and the household were not simply a matter of political theory in early modern Europe, they also shaped law codes and their enforcement. Rulers intent on increasing and centralizing their own authority supported legal and institutional changes that enhanced the power of men over the women and children in their own families. In France, for example, a series of laws were enacted between 1556 and 1789 that increased both paternal and state control of marriage. Parental consent was required for marriage, and severe penalties, including capital punishment, were prescribed for minors who married against their parents' wishes. (Minors were defined as men under thirty and women under twenty-five.) Marriages without parental consent were defined as *rapt* (abduction), even if they had involved no violence (such cases were termed *rapt de seduction*). Though in actuality they were not executed, young people who defied their parents were sometimes imprisoned by what were termed *lettres de cachet*, documents that families obtained from royal officials authorizing the imprisonment without trial of a family member who was seen as a source of dishonor. *Lettres de cachet* were also used against young people who refused to go into convents or monasteries when their families wished them to, or against individuals whose behavior was regarded as in some way scandalous, such as wives whose husbands suspected them of adultery or men from prominent families who engaged in homosexual activities; this practice was often abused, and individuals imprisoned for years if their families refused to agree to their release. These laws and practices were proposed and supported by French officials because they increased their personal authority within their own families, and simultaneously increased the authority of the state vis-à-vis the Catholic church, which had required at least the nominal consent of both parties for a valid marriage. This "family/state compact," as the historian Sarah Hanley terms it, dramatically lessened women's rights to control their own persons and property; these marriage laws would be one of the first things that French women's rights advocates in the nineteenth and twentieth centuries worked to change.[25]

The authority of husbands over their wives was rarely disputed in the sixteenth and seventeenth centuries, which was an important reason why women were not included in discussions of political rights; because married women were legally dependent, they could not be politically independent persons, just as servants, apprentices, or tenants could not. Thus even the most eloquent defenders of women, such as Agrippa of Nettesheim, did not suggest practical ways to increase women's political rights and simply avoided the issue of marriage when promoting women's equality or superiority. The strongest supporters of a queen's right to rule, such as Thomas Smith, did not suggest extending political rights to other women: "In which consideration also do we reject women, as those whom nature hath made to keepe home and to nourish their familie and children, and not to medle with matters abroade, nor to beare office in a citie or commonwealth no more than children and infantes."[26]

Husbandly authority was not simply a matter of theory. In France men occasionally used *lettres de cachet* as a means of solving marital disputes, convincing officials that family honor demanded the imprisonment of their wives, while in Italy and Spain a "dis-

Fig. 4 Hans Schäufelein, *Der Windelwascher* (*Diaper Washer*), Woodcut to lost poem Ho, Ho Diaper Washer by Hans Sachs, *c.* 1536, 250 × 218 mm (9⅞ × 8⅝ in.), Kunstsammlungen der Veste Coburg, Germany

obedient" wife could be sent to a convent or house of refuge for repentant prostitutes.[27] Courts generally held that a husband had the right to beat his wife in order to correct her behavior as long as this was not extreme, with a common standard being that he did not draw blood, or that the diameter of the stick he used did not exceed that of his thumb. (This is the origin of the term "rule of thumb.") A husband accused of abuse in court was generally simply admonished to behave better, and only on a third or fourth court appearance might stricter punishment be set. If the wife had left the household she was ordered to return, though there are cases in many jurisdictions where this eventually led to a wife's death at the hands of her husband. The reverse situation, in which a wife killed her husband, was much rarer, but the few cases that did exist fascinated people and were often retold in illustrated pamphlets and broadsheets with titles such as *Murther, Murther. Or, a Bloody Relation How Anne Hamton ... by Poyson Murthered Her Deare Husband* (London, 1641). In England killing a husband was legally defined as "petty treason" and punishable by death at the stake.[28]

Wives dominating husbands were connected with other ways in which the expected hierarchy might be overturned—the unlearned leading the learned, the young controlling the old—in both learned and popular literature and popular festivals. Carnival plays frequently portrayed domineering wives in pants and hen-pecked husbands washing diapers alongside of professors in dunce caps and peasants riding princes (fig. 4). These figures appear in woodcuts and engravings, and in songs, stories, and poems.

Men and women involved in relationships in which the women were thought to have power—an older woman who married a younger man, or a woman who scolded her husband—were often subjected to public ridicule, with bands of neighbors shouting insults and banging sticks and pans in their disapproval.[29] Women were clearly understood to have authority within the household, but such rituals, along with laws, family records, and theoretical discussions, tried to make it clear that this authority was supposed to be derivative, a result of the woman's status as wife or widow of the male household head. This was emphasized by referring to her as "wife" rather than "mother" even in legal documents describing her relations with her children, and by family records, especially in Italy, that include only the male line.[30]

CONCLUSIONS

Women's authority in the state and the household in early modern Europe was thus simultaneously accepted and questioned, necessary and problematic. Of all the ways in which society was hierarchically arranged—class, age, rank, race, occupation—gender was regarded as the most "natural" and therefore the most important to defend, but it also cut across all those other hierarchies, making the occasional reversal of the normal gender order an essential part of the stability of every other hierarchy. Despite arguments by Knox and others that female rulers were "monsters in nature," Elizabeth's and Isabella's right to rule was affirmed, as was that of many other queens as well as lesser noblewomen in the smaller states of Italy and the Holy Roman Empire. A married woman's authority over her children (including her sons) and her servants (including her male servants) was supported in legal theory and in actual court decisions, though perhaps not quite as vigorously as that of her husband over these individuals or over her.

Along with socially sanctioned, though problematic, authority in the state and the household, women also had other types of power in early modern Europe. Wealthy and middle-class women provided patronage for writers, artists, architects, scientists, and musicians, often in the form of commissions. They exerted political patronage, helping or hindering men's political careers. Through the arrangement of marriages, they established ties between influential families; through letters or the spreading of rumors, they shaped networks of opinion; through giving advice and founding institutions, they shaped policy; through participation in riots and disturbances, they demonstrated the weakness of male authority structures. Women of all social classes exerted emotional and sexual power—which sometimes led to their claiming authority as well—in marriage, and always provided a topic for moralists, preachers, and writers. As this exhibition makes clear, concerns about women's exercise of both authority and power found visual as well as verbal expression in early modern Europe, making even the most positive portrayals of powerful women often ambiguous and multivalent.

NOTES

1 "Enuma Elish," from Heidel 1942, p. 42.

2 For an insightful analysis of the role of Lucretia in the Renaissance, see Jed 1989.

3 Greenblatt 1980.

4 Castiglione 1959.

5 Kuchta 1993.

6 General discussions of the debate include: Maclean 1980; Joan Kelly, "Early Feminist Theory and the *Querelle des Femmes*, 1400–1789" in Kelly 1984, pp. 65–109; and Henderson and McManus 1985.

7 De Pizan 1982; Agrippa 1996; O'Malley 1996; Fonte 1997; Marinella 2000.

8 Bodin 1606; Joseph Swetnam's *The Arraignment of Lewd, Idle, Froward, and Unconstant Women*, 1615, and several replies are collected in Swetnam 1996.

9 Edward Gosynhill, for example, is the likely author of both a humorous attack on women, *The Schoolhouse of Women*, London 1541, and a sober defense, *The Praise of All Women*, London 1542, both excerpted in Henderson and McManus 1985, pp. 136–70.

10 Woodbridge (1984) argues that it is a literary exercise, and Jordan (1990b) that it is a serious matter.

11 Studies of visual representations of the debate include Matthews Grieco 1989; Moxey 1989; and Bottigheimer 1995.

12 The debate about female rulers has been analyzed in Jordan 1990 and Shephard 1994.

13 Queen Elizabeth I, Tilbury speech, quoted in Teague 1987, p. 542. Whether Elizabeth actually gave this speech has been debated in Frye 1992 and Green 1997.

14 For cultural studies of Elizabeth, see Montrose 1983; Berry 1989; Levin 1994; King 1990; Frye 1993.

15 ffolliott 1997; K. Crawford (forthcoming); Johnson 1997; Marrow 1982.

16 Merrick 1988.

17 Machiavelli 1980, p. 149.

18 *Political Works of James I*, 1965, pp. 272–73, 307.

19 Merrick 1993.

20 Jean Bodin, *Six Books of the Republic*, translated and quoted in Fauré 1991, p. 40.

21 Doran 1996.

22 There is a very large literature on Protestant ideas about the family and the effects of the Protestant Reformation on women and family life. Good places to begin are Todd 1987; Roper 1989; P. Crawford 1993; Carlson 1994; Harrington 1995; and Hendrix 1995.

23 Matheson 1995; James 1687.

24 Relational feminism is analyzed in Offen 2000.

25 Hanley 1989; Hanley 1997.

26 Smith 1583, sig. D2r.

27 Perry 1990, pp. 53–60; Cohen 1992, pp. 77–80.

28 Studies of domestic violence include: Boose 1991; Hunt 1992; Amussen 1994; Dolan 1994; Ferraro 1995; Gowing 1996. The pamphlet *Murther, Murther* is mentioned in Gowing 1996, p. 202.

29 N. Davis 1975.

30 Klapisch-Zuber 1985, pp. 284–85.

4
CLAUDE DERUET
French, c. 1588–1660
Departure of the Amazons, from a cycle of Battles of the Amazons

1620s
Oil on canvas
50.8 × 66 cm (20 × 26 in.)
Lent by The Metropolitan Museum of Art, New York, Bequest of Harry G. Sperling, 1971

5
CLAUDE DERUET
French, c. 1588–1660
Triumph of the Amazons, from a cycle of Battles of the Amazons

1620s
Oil on canvas
51.4 × 66 cm (20¼ × 26 in.)
Lent by The Metropolitan Museum of Art, New York, Bequest of Harry G. Sperling, 1971

These two paintings originally belonged to a cycle of four paintings of Amazon battle scenes; the two remaining works, both titled *Battle of the Amazons and the Greeks*, reside today in the Musée Jeanne d'Aboville, La Fère. Deruet worked for most of his career as the court painter and director of festivals for the Dukes of Lorraine. He probably painted the Metropolitan/La Fère cycle in his early years of service, not long after returning from a number of years of study in Italy.

6

GEORG PENCZ

German, c. 1500–1550

Samson and Delilah

c. 1531–32
Engraving
39 × 50 mm (1½ × 2 in.)
Ann Arbor, University of Michigan
Museum of Art, The W. Hawkins
Ferry Fund, 1999

Samson, one of the judges of ancient Israel, was famous for his great strength. Delilah, his lover, came from the Philistines, Israel's enemy, and was promised a great deal of money by her people to deceive him. She persuaded Samson to reveal that the source of his great strength was his hair, which had not been cut since his birth. While Samson slept, Delilah cut Samson's locks, and the great hero awoke to find himself weakened and helpless before his enemies. Pencz's engraving accords with the Old Testament as it depicts Samson lying with his head in Delilah's lap, underscoring the notion that it was by her feminine wiles that Delilah was able to overcome Samson.

7

JAN GOSSAERT,
called MABUSE

Flemish, c. 1478–1532

Adam and Eve

c. 1525
Black chalk
628 × 460 mm
(24¾ × 18⅛ in.)
Providence, The Museum of Art,
Rhode Island School of Design,
Walter H. Kimball Fund

Gossaert's drawing stresses that the origin of sexual knowledge was involved in the Fall of Man, and also that Eve was to blame for this discovery. Eve's frank reach toward Adam's genitals, and the pair's intertwining limbs make explicit the sexual outcome of Eve's plucking of the fruit. Adam appears as the victim of both the alluring Eve and the serpent who descends from the tree: Eve's gesture of aggression is paralleled by the flick of the serpent's tongue, which brushes Adam's left hand.

8, 9, 10

FRANÇOIS CHAUVEAU

French 1613–1676

Deborah, Tomyris, and Judith in Jacques Du Bosc, La femme héroïque, ou, Les héroïnes comparées avec les héros en toutes sortes de vertus. Et plusieurs reflexions morales à la fin de chaque comparaison, Paris, Antoine de Sommaville and Augustin Courbé, 1645

Engraving

180 × 125 mm

(7 × 5 in.) image

Saint Bonaventure, Saint Bonaventure University, Friedsam Memorial Library, Franciscan Institute Collection

Jacques Du Bosc's *La femme héroïque,* one of the most important feminist works of the seventeenth century, mounts the argument that women possess the same virtues as men. Eight pairs of famous women and men from biblical and ancient history are discussed, their characters and accomplishments compared. The illustrations of the heroines and heroes, which open on facing pages, often make a point of their equality through formal means, in the repetition of gestures, or in mirrored compositions.

The comparison of Tomyris, queen of the Massagetae, and Cyrus the Great, has perhaps a touch of irony, since it was in battle against Tomyris's forces that Cyrus met his death, and it is in fact his decapitated head that is being presented to the queen. The heroine and the hero strike mirroring poses, and both are represented on battlefields, although Tomyris does not appear as a warrior queen in Herodotus's account.

Deborah, prophet and judge of ancient Israel, at whose instigation the Israelites mounted a successful campaign against the Canaanites, is compared to Joshua, a great warrior and leader of the Israelites who captured Jericho and conquered Canaan. The biblical passages in both inscriptions mention the heavens' seeming approval of their deeds, thus further cementing the parallel between the two.

A long-established tradition exists comparing Judith to David. Both figures defeated and decapitated vanquished foes— Holofernes and Goliath—of much greater physical strength, and in both cases, their victories were interpreted as demonstrations of divine favor, and of the righteousness of their deeds.

HEROIQVE L.I. 91

DEBORA VICTORIEVSE DES CANANEENS

Les Estoilles demeurant dans leur Ordre et leur Cours accoustumé ont bataillé contre Sisara. au liure des Iuges Chap. 5.

HEROIQVE L.III. 183

THOMYRIS VICTORIEVSE DE CYRVS.

Boy maintenant a ton ayse du sang humain, dont tu as esté si alteré. Herodote. l. 1.

F.C. in et fe.

Vne femme Iuifue a ietté la Confusion
dans la maison du Roy Nabuchodonosor
au·l· de Iudith·

II

HENDRICK GOLTZIUS
Dutch, 1558–1617
After BARTHOLOMÄUS
SPRANGER
Flemish, 1546–1611

**Judith with the Head
of Holofernes**

c. 1585
Engraving
147 mm (5⅞ in.) diam.,
cut on borderline
Lent by the Museum of Fine Arts,
Boston, Harvey D. Parker Collection

Judith holds Holofernes's head
aloft in a militaristic gesture
of triumph. This pose, in
conjunction with her muscular
torso, her codpiece-like drapery,
and the prominent hilt of her
sword, lend Judith's figure an
androgynous appearance. Yet
androgyny was also common in
art associated with the court of
Rudolf II in Prague, where
Goltzius made prints after court
painter Spranger.

12

PARIS BORDONE
Italian, 1500–1571

Athena Scorning the Advances of Hephaestus

c. 1555–60
Oil on canvas
139.4 × 127.7 cm
(54⅞ × 50¼ in.)
Columbia, Museum of Art
and Archaeology, University of
Missouri-Columbia, Gift of the
Samuel H. Kress Foundation

In this elegantly choreographed
work, Bordone has created a
titillating play of dominance and
submission between Hephaestus
(Vulcan) and Athena (Minerva).
Hephaestus is the aggressor in
his attempted restraint of Athena,
but his gesture is also one of
palpable desperation; his exposed
backside and his unstable pose
make him appear vulnerable,
more so perhaps than the
armored goddess, who, looking
down with apparent displeasure,
draws her arm back in an
ambiguous gesture that can be
interpreted both as self-protective
withdrawal and perhaps as
preparation for a backhanded
swipe.

AEGID ROUSSELET
French, n.d.
and ABRAHAM BOSSE
French, 1602–1676
After **CLAUDE VIGNON**
French, 1593–1670
Zenobia in Pierre Le Moyne, *La Gallerie des femmes fortes*, Paris, Antoine de Sommaville, 1647

Engraving with etching
340 × 215 mm (13⅜ × 8⅜ in.)
New Haven, The Beinecke Rare Book and Manuscript Library, Yale University

Pierre Le Moyne's *La Gallerie des femmes fortes* is a "collection" of twenty famous women from ancient, biblical, and recent history. A chapter is devoted to each woman, containing a narrative of her life, and a moral commentary on the virtues the woman exemplifies. The *Gallerie* is dedicated to Anne of Austria, who was queen regent at the time of its publication.

Zenobia was queen of the Roman colony of Palmyra, in present-day Syria, from A.D. 267/8 to 272, after her husband was assassinated. As regent for her young son, she led a military conquest of Asia Minor, and declared independence from Rome, although she was eventually defeated and taken captive to Rome.

ZENOBIE *Reyne des Palmyreniens, victorieuse des Roys et des Lyons, aguerrit Enfans à la chasse: et les dresse par son exemple à la vaillance et à la victoire.* Trebellius
Vignon inuent.   *Mariette escud. cum pri*

CAMME. *Princesse de Galatie, victorieuse de l'Amour et de la Mort, fait vn sacrifice fidelité et de vengeance à l'Ombre de Sinnate son Mary.* Plutar. de Mulierum virtutibus.

Vignon inuent. Mariette excud. cum

14

AEGID ROUSSELET
French, n.d.
and ABRAHAM BOSSE
French, 1602–1676
After CLAUDE VIGNON
French, 1593–1670
Camma in Pierre
Le Moyne, La Gallerie
des femmes fortes, Paris,
Antoine de
Sommaville, 1647

Engraving with etching
340 × 215 mm (13⅜ × 8⅜ in.)
New Haven, The Beinecke Rare Book
and Manuscript Library, Yale
University

Camma, a heroine from ancient history, sacrificed her own life in order to avenge the death of her husband, Sinatus. In order to deceive his murderer Synorix, she agreed to marry him, and then proceeded to poison him and herself during their wedding ceremony.

15
ISRAHEL VAN
MECKENEM
Dutch, before 1450–1503
The Angry Wife,
from the series
Scenes of Daily Life

c. 1495/1503
Engraving
167 × 111 mm
(6⅝ × 4⅜ in.)
Chapel Hill, Ackland Art Museum,
The University of North Carolina at
Chapel Hill, Ackland Fund

Representations of women
dominating their husbands were
a common carnivalesque theme,
along with others that similarly
inverted conventional power
relations. Here, a woman beats
her husband with her distaff, a
symbol of woman's traditionally
subservient role; the man has
been stripped of his trousers
(a symbol of mastery of the
family), which now lie on the
ground beside him. Like the
power of women topos, these
scenes of inversion were often
presented as comic, although
the seriousness of the ultimate
message—the necessity of
maintaining male dominance
over women—was not obscured.

16

MASTER MZ
(MATTHÄUS
ZAISINGER?)
German, active *c.* 1500
Phyllis Riding Aristotle

c. 1500
Engraving
182 × 132 mm (7¼ × 5¼ in.)
sheet, trimmed on platemark
Lent by the Museum of Fine Arts,
Boston, Stephen Bullard Memorial
Fund and William A. Sargent Fund

Among the most popular of the
power of women subjects was the
story of Aristotle and Phyllis.
After warning his pupil
Alexander the Great about
the dangers of paying too
much attention to his wife
(or mistress), Phyllis, Aristotle
himself began to desire her. In
exchange for her acquiescence,
she demanded that Aristotle wear
a bridle and let her ride on his
back. The story is meant to show
that even Aristotle, who
ostensibly exemplified men's
superior reasoning capacity,
could be reduced to the position
of a beast by his desire for a
woman.

School of LUCAS
CRANACH
German, 1472–1553
Lucretia

16th century
Oil on panel
47 × 34.2 cm (18½ × 13½ in.)
University of California, Berkeley Art
Museum, Bequest of Alfred Bach,
1983

In the legendary history of early
Rome, the virtuous noblewoman
Lucretia committed suicide after
being raped by Sextus, the son of
the tyrant Tarquin. Like many
representations of Lucretia, this
painting depicts her as beautiful
and seductive, suggesting that
she was at fault for her violation.
Moreover, the painting's portrait-
like focus on the moment of
death, its emphasis on sensual
materials, and Lucretia's
titillating dishabille seem to
offer the viewer an eroticized
experience of death itself.
Lucas Cranach and his followers
executed many paintings of
famous women from history and
legend, particularly those known
for their deadly charms.

18

ANONYMOUS

16ᵗʰ century

Portrait of Queen Elizabeth I

c. 1559

Oil on panel

36 × 22.8 cm (14 × 9 in.)

Collection of Christopher Foley

This hitherto unpublished portrait of Elizabeth I is intriguing for its depiction of the young queen in a sumptuous interior. The queen is contained, even cloistered, much like the Virgin Mary in the enclosed garden or in scenes of the Annunciation to the Virgin. Elizabeth was eventually to negotiate with court artists different self-presentations in which she projected herself as a virgin queen, replete with symbols of chastity, imperialism, and statecraft.

POSVI DEVM ADIVTOREM MEVM

Mirtæ ons
MIserICorDIæ.

SEMPER EADEM

Nata Gronoviciæ
anno Christi
MDXXXIII·
6. Id. Sept.

ELISABET D.G. ANGLIAE, FRANCIAE, HIBERNIAE, ET VERGINIAE REGINA,
FIDEI CHRISTIANAE PROPVGNATRIX ACERRIMA. NVNC IN DNO REQVIESCENS.

Virginis os habitusque geris, divina virago,
Sed supra sexum dotes animusque virilem;
Quod sæpe altarom docuit rerum exitus ingens;
Unde tibi et Regni populi debere fatentur,
Christiadumque cohors, odio pugnantur ut hostes

Das in Semiramiden Babylon super æthera tollat,
Efferat et Didona suam Sidonia tellus,
Gens Es thren Iudæa, Camillam Volsca propago,
Aut Constantini matrem Byzantion ingens;

Isaac Olivier
effigiabat.
Crispin van de Passe
incidebat.

19
CRISPIN VAN DE
PASSE THE ELDER
Dutch, c. 1565–1637
After ISAAC OLIVER
French, active in England,
1558/68–1617
Portrait of Queen
Elizabeth I

c. 1603
Engraving
345 × 225 mm (13⅝ × 8⅞ in.)
Cincinnati, Cincinnati Art Museum,
Bequest of Herbert Greer French

Crispin van de Passe's memorial
portrait of Elizabeth I was a
widely disseminated and copied
image. The coat of arms, her
crown, orb, and scepter refer
to Elizabeth's secular authority,
while the motto "Posui Deum
Adiutorem Meum" (I have
made God my help) and the
iconography of the sword of
justice resting on the Bible allude
to her role as a divine
instrument. The inscription
below hails Elizabeth as *virgin*
and *divine virago*, and compares
her to the ancient and biblical
heroines Semiramis, Dido,
Esther, and Camilla

20

CRISPIN VAN DE
PASSE THE ELDER
Dutch, c. 1565–1637
*Portrait of Queen
Elizabeth I*

1596
Engraving
324 × 254 mm (12¾ × 10 in.)
London, The British Museum,
Department of Prints and Drawings

Elizabeth I, sumptuously clad
and holding scepter and orb,
stands between two columns.
These refer to the Pillars of
Hercules, rocks that were
believed to mark the limits of
the ancient world. The columns
and the ships symbolic of
England's maritime dominancy—
recalling England's defeat of the
Armada in 1588—refer to the
Queen's imperialist ambitions.
Perched on one column is the
phoenix, symbolic of chastity; on
the other is the pelican, symbolic
of charity.

ELIZABETA D. G. ANGLIÆ. FRANCIÆ. HIBERNIÆ. ET VERGINIÆ
REGINA CHRISTIANAE FIDEI VNICVM PROPVGNACVLVM.

Immortalis honos Regum, cui non tulit ætas   Queis ipsæ tantum superant reliqua omnia regna,
      Ulla prior, veniens nec feret ulla parem,   Quantum tu maior Regibus es reliquis,
Sospite quo nunquam terras habitare Britannas   Viue precor felix tanti in moderamine regni,
      Desinet alma Quies, Iustitia atque Fides,   Dum tibi Rex Regum cælica regna paret.

In honorem serenissimæ Suæ Maiestatis hanc effigiem fieri curabat Ioannes Woutnelius belga. Anno 1596.

21

ANTOINE CARON

French, c. 1521–c. 1599

*Catherine de' Medici
Receiving the Polish
Ambassadors in the
Tuileries Gardens*

1573

Brown ink, brown wash, and white
gouache over black chalk

342 × 490 mm

(13½ × 19¼ in.)

Cambridge, Fogg Art Museum,
Harvard University Art Museums,
Gift of Mr. and Mrs. Winslow Ames

Caron's drawing depicts a festival
put on by the court of Catherine
de' Medici to welcome the Polish
royal entourage. The visit took
place in September 1573, after
Catherine's diplomacy resulted in
Henri of Anjou's being crowned
king of King of Poland in June
of the same year. Such festivals,
which often included elaborate
performances, served multiple
functions in establishing and
maintaining relations between
rulers. They were simultaneously
demonstrations of the largesse of
the host, as well as displays of the
wealth and power of each party.

22

JEAN-BAPTISTE MASSÉ
French, 1687–1767
After PETER PAUL
RUBENS
Flemish, 1577–1640

*Marie de' Medici as
Minerva*

1708?
Engraving
510 × 358 mm
(20 × 14 in.) plate,
682 × 502 mm
(26⅞ × 19¾ in.) sheet
Lent by The Metropolitan Museum
of Art, New York, Gift of Georgiana
W. Sargent, in memory of John
Osborne Sargent, 1924

Massé's print reproduces
Rubens's painting of Marie de'
Medici as Minerva in his famous
cycle on Marie's life and reign.
Although the engraving's
inscription identifies the figure
as "Marie de' Medici in the form
of Minerva, goddess of the arts,"
the attributes that commonly
link Minerva with the arts are
conspicuously absent. Instead,
those that identify her as the
goddess of war are emphasized.
It is uncertain whether Marie is
to be understood as Bellona,
Minerva's more bellicose aspect,
or as a symbol of a peaceful end
to a just war.

23

BERNARD PICARD
French, 1673–1733
After JEAN-MARC
NATTIER
French, 1685–1766
After PETER PAUL
RUBENS
Flemish, 1577–1640
The Felicity of the
Regency, 1704, in
La Gallerie du Palais
du Luxembourg, Paris,
Duchange, 1710

Engraving
500 × 355 mm
(19⅝ × 14 in.) plate
New York, The New York Public
Library

In this engraving after one of
Rubens's paintings in the great
cycle glorifying the life of Marie
de' Medici, the diademed queen
is shown at her most regal. She is
represented as Astraea (the virgin
goddess identified with justice)
with a pair of scales in her right
hand. Other divine figures,
including Minerva, Saturn, and
Abundance, accompany her in
this commemoration of the
golden age of her regency.

Rubens pinxit   J. M. Nattier delineavit B. Picard Sculpsit

La Felicité de la Regence

L'heureux Gouvernement de la Reine est icy marqué par l'équité, par l'abondance, par les sciences et par les arts.
La Reine dans son trône tient une balance à la main, et represente cette vertu, qui distribue les recompenses, et les
châtimens selon les merites. Elle est accompagnée de Minerve et de l'amour. D'un côté la Medisance, l'Ignorance et
l'Envie sont terrassées par les Genies des beaux arts, et de l'autre on voit le tems qui conduit la France au siecle d'or.

A Paris chez le Sr Nattier Peintre de l'Academie Royale rue Frementeau. Avec Privilege du Roy.

Women as the Topic

MIEKE BAL

When I first looked at the images selected for inclusion in this exhibition, all I could see was a collection of two-dimensional, far-away representations that were completely alien to me. The images were so historical, so unengaging as artistic works, that I was practically unable to see them. They appeared to me an odd mix of two different kinds of images—mythical and historical. They seemed so very diverse. But then, slowly, the myth emerged from within the history. Queen Elizabeth I receded into myth as Tomyris, Judith, and Jael became her next-door neighbors.

First I will estrange or "denaturalize" the thematic exhibition as a concept, through cases where "images of women"—women as the topic—were selected on the basis of the power attributed to them—women at the top. I will do this by pointing out two aspects of this combination of images that are by no means logically consistent. My aim is to foreground complexities at the heart of what might seem simple: a thematic selection. I will then argue that things are not what they appear to be. Rather than reiterating a deeply problematic tendency in a male-dominated culture, a thematic exhibition can, under certain conditions, critically engage with the fantasies underlying that culture. I will propose that this exhibition succeeds in avoiding the problematic aspects of such a thematic show—women as the topic—because it makes the semi-automatic association with women at the top less "natural."

TWO SPECULATIONS

It does this by making things strange, through two interventions. A first strange feature of the show is the presence of the likes of Queen Elizabeth in this sort of collection of mythical women figures who take power over men. She was not a sudden figment of the frightened male imagination but just happened to be born to power. And she is not a mythical but a historical figure. Or is she? The question, here, is how historical women in positions of power tie in with the imaginary paranoia about mythical figures. Just born to power, Elizabeth existed, did her job, and died. During her lifetime she had already become the object of a visual fascination that extended beyond the traditional portraiture of royal figures.[1]

Opposite: Rembrandt van Rijn, *Lucretia*, 1666 (fig. 13, detail)

The second, much more disturbing surprise is the presence of the figure of Lucretia. This figure is the quintessential victim, triply victimized by men. She is raped, she kills herself, and then her body is put on public display and used for political aims. How does she end up in this grouping, and in other exhibitions devoted to "strong women," "women who ruled," "women at the top"? And not only in exhibitions but in the visual culture of the time—to the extent that we see beautiful (Venus), dangerous (Judith), and victimized (Lucretia) women together in a single representation (pl. 24)? I will try to connect the question of mythification of real power with the hyperbolic paranoia that turns victims into henchmen when women are the power-brokers.

While staying away from psychoanalytic interpretations, which are a bit too predictable when it comes to this topic, I will speculate on the social meanings of such representations of women in power. For I wonder what it means that beauty (Helen of Troy) (pl. 25),[2] when perceived as desirable (Venus) (pl. 26), diminishes the subject of desire in his own eyes, to the point of willing a suicidal exposure to castration and murder (Holofernes) (pl. 28). In reference to the contest for the golden apple, plate 25 shows Helen offering her breasts like apples on a plate. Venus is frequently depicted at her toilet, so that she offers an opportunity for a nude, combined with a hint at women's narcissism because she is bound to look into a mirror, as in Velázquez's famous Rokeby Venus from 1648, in the National Gallery, London. The mirror required for the idea of toilet also allows the clever device of showing the "real" Venus from the side, as if she is innocently unaware of our gaze, yet in her mirror image, a colluding look at the viewer. Plate 28, part of a thematic series, is explicitly presented since it is part of a scene of "cases" of women in power positions. If we take such combinations seriously, as significant statements about the cultural imagination, we must conclude that the problem these images contend with is the nature of desire itself. Desire is thus reduced to power struggle, and this whether the desire is fulfilled, as in seduction, turned into violence, as in rape, or repelled, as in the institution of virginity.

But this speculation only goes halfway toward an explanation. For it begs the question of why these negative gender attitudes lead to a properly visual fascination. Fascination is more than just excessive interest: it is a combination of extreme attraction and repulsion, the impossibility of staying away from what frightens and yet seduces. At least, this is fascination according to the age-old model of Medusa.[3] My second speculation concerns this visual obsession.

As a social occurrence, fascination is as necessary as it is problematic. Women, I speculate, cannot be contemplated at all unless within such an outward projection of men's fear of their own desire, yet they must be, for looking arouses and sustains desire. Hence, looking at women must be "naturalized" in specific narrative fantasies justifying the fear-within-the-desire that characterizes the male terror of their own bodies. The abundance of images of these stereotypical interpretations of women that reduce the possible social roles of women to sexualized ones, displays, in fact, the map of women's visibility.

With women's visibility, I mean, quite literally, that women cannot, a priori, be simply looked at and seen. Questioning that ordinary social existence entails inquiry into the strange situation in which concrete women are hidden behind the veil of Woman, a male-constructed image that is a projection screen of men's own fears: women cannot be seen or contemplated without instilling horror and anxiety; yet they must be seen, constantly, even kept under surveillance. Only power can be so feared. In the end, then, an exhibition on women—where women are on show (women as the topic)—is, by definition, an exhibition of women who rule (women at the top). When women are the topic, visually, they are by definition "on top."

WOMEN IN VISUAL CULTURE

The visibility of women: how can it be doubted in a culture where women are supposed to dress up for seduction and conquest, and where, as early second-wave feminists have complained, the only role for women is to be the object of male desire?[4] The problem here, the oppressive, stereotypifying cultural gesture, is to put women on display. The gaze is an instrument of surveillance; the eroticized gaze, an instrument of appropriation. Women on display can do no harm; they become mute objects.

We are no longer so naïve, or so blind, as to think that women are only objects, or that only men can desire women on the basis of their visual representation. Yet something of this simple idea sticks. This is because the pin-up quality of "images of women" flaunts a paradox. Exuberant imagery of women suggests not that they are invisible but that they are over-visible. True enough. I suggest, however, that this hypervisibility continues to go hand in hand with invisibility: if you are trained to see women all around you—real ones, but more importantly, women on display, on posters, on television, or on other instruments of visual culture—in other words, if they are over- or hypervisible, they are more easily overlooked, and become invisible. Displaying female bodies is an effective strategy to maintain their invisibility. Hence, it remains a bit of a shock to realize that the entire history of art can be construed as one long struggle with the paradox of female (in)visibility. The "official story"—the one promoted by early feminist protest—is simple. The nude, it has been argued, makes up for the invisibility of female genitalia and the horror this alleged absence inspired in those equipped with a more cumbersome but at least visible identifying "thing."

But this story, as I said, is a bit too simple. Let me juxtapose it with an "unofficial" one that is a bit more complicated, for three distinct reasons, all implied in this exhibition. The first is institutional, the second structural, the third representational. First, the images are presented within an institutional context. Their perception is "impure" because the images presented cannot be understood on the basis of what they show alone. They are part of a long trail of cultural "things," the best known of which are stories. For example, the tankard cited here as plate 24 did not emerge out of the blue. For the figures of Judith and Venus it had models, which, by chance, have been identified.[5] Users of the object whose fingers caressed the image of Judith when they drank their beer did not have to know this, of course. But they were used to seeing Judiths, and understood, in an unreflected kind of knowledge of everyday life, what her representation meant. They might, when they got a bit drunk, make jokes about the fear she stood for. Hence, the more complex story I am putting forward is an "impure" one because it contaminates the crime scene, the official shrine to visual art that art museums are. As a collection of objects, this exhibition and its stated theme do not accommodate the domain of visuality as "essential," as essentially different from the domain of words.

The sheer bringing together of all this material helps us to see how images cannot be seen in isolation. If we are to understand the images in this exhibition, we must let go of the desire to understand them, at first glance, as a coherent set. The combination, or "collocation" (the speaking together), of reigning queens and killing monsters from mythology breaks open the boundaries of our traditional take on what an image can be as "art." In other words, to understand this exhibition it is imperative to endorse a notion of what this exhibition symptomatically presents, as lying beyond art history. The groupings here, to which the thematic endeavor remains resistant (many categories overlap of necessity), tell an "impure" story of things visual; a story not of art history but of visual culture.

It is also an "impure" story because it decomposes the simple, "official" story in its very structure. The latter, with its gender-based binary opposition as the ground for complaint—women are put on display for male delectation, women are passive, men active, and so on—sticks to the structure of thought in which subject (he who sees) and object (she who is the object of the gaze) are systemically opposed. From that opposition, to the one between colonizer and colonized, between torturer and victim, is but one step. The object of the allegedly male gaze—perversely made over-visible because only staring at her can neutralize the horror of her invisibility—must be turned into, precisely, a still image, as dead as a stillborn baby. This raises the question of who, in this dynamic, is really the subject, and who the object? Perhaps this stark opposition is fascinating because it undercuts binary opposition itself as a reliable structure.

And lastly it is an "impure" story because it does not respect the division of the domain of culture into "reality" and "fiction." The combination of "women who ruled"— in historical reality—and figures who killed men—in ancient stories—illuminates this impurity, and asks for a concept that does not divide culture into "true" and "false." As a mediating term I adopt "myth." But the meaning of this term can only be approximated.

Myth has frequently been seen as either ideology or ancient ethnography. But, lest we fall back into such rehearsed definitions of myth, the term is better off suspended, and then mobilized, in order to be fleshed out through confrontation with these images.[6] I take the presence of cultural myths, in whatever form—stories or images, for adults or for children, in books or on tankards—seriously, as cultural reality. For the time being, "myth" stands for the reality of a culture where imagery informs social relations as much as the other way around, and where words and images, sounds and smells are all indistinguishably real and imaginary. "Myth," in other words, is for reality what "queer" is for gays and "witch" is for women: an appropriated term to explain and thus, potentially, eradicate what the unreflected earlier use of the word-as-insult can only perpetuate. Here, the incompatibility of power and women is fought out in a contest of vision.

These three "impurities"—of institution, structure, and reality domains—make utter sense of what seemed to be, at first sight, an oddity. Instead, however, the exhibition makes a powerful case for the visual self-undermining or "deconstruction"—if that word may be used here—of precisely those aspects of the "official story" of the slander on women in those predominant representations that inspired early feminists' complaints.

Fig. 5 Master BG (German, late 16th c.), *Judith and Holofernes*, ivory, 203 mm (8 in.), Lawrence, Spencer Museum of Art, The University of Kansas

This exhibition displays everyday records of the myth that the three "impurities" expose. It presents these records as cultural elements that "act" (hence, as agents) through the figurations of the myth in specific narratives, narratives that emerge for reasons that may be political but that overstay that motivation. I have to limit myself to one example. No myth establishes the connection between women's power and the question of their visibility more aptly than that of Judith.[7]

It is no coincidence that Judith ends up on coins, sculptures, household utensils (such as the tankard in plate 24), and, of course, paintings. These representations are no more confined to "art" than they are to modern museums. At the time these objects were made, they were part of a culture that was made up of such things. Sculptures, like Donatello's from c. 1455 at the Piazza della Signoria in Florence, stood, and often still stand, in public places.[8] People walking to their workplace, maids and housewives going shopping, would pass Donatello's sculpture every day, walk around it, some seeing the back with the raised arm, some the Christ-like Holofernes only. The Judith images might also be grasped by a warm hand, as happened in the case of the small ivory sculptures that slowly became smoother from being handled and caressed (fig. 5). One could actually touch, feel, and caress the smooth ivory, and thus the tangle of legs and arms at the bottom of the sculpture. Coins became smooth from going from hand to hand. Engravings were in books read by men, to women and children. What were they thinking, when the story was accompanied by etchings such as this one, part of a series (pl. 29)? And, in the richer households, paintings of Judith hung on the walls, where they impressed the visitors.

We are so used to seeing paintings in museums only that it may be a bit hard to imagine what they would do in a private home. Inhabitants of a house in an Italian city would sit by the fire at night and look at the heroic interpretation by one of the female artists of their time, Elisabetta Sirani (pl. 30). This image shows Judith and her maid, returning to Bethulia after a job well done with trumpets of triumph. Others looked at the beautiful widow, an emblem of female beauty and virtue combined, not at the usual seductress who murdered a man, as in the painting by Massimo Stanzione (fig. 6). Still others saw an old woman together with a bare-breasted, sexualized younger woman, plotting fateful events. But many more saw, day by day, how this mythical woman figure held the head of her victim, as in this painting, by an artist who was also a woman, but who identified more easily with her culture, male dominated as it was, than with her sex (pl. 32). Or, worse, when returning home from a busy day full of aggravation, the lord of the house would catch the bitch in the act, first on his way home at the piazza, then again on his living room wall, before turning the pages of his book, where she appeared again, doing her trick.

Judith is a powerful figure who did not rule, like a queen, but who undid the power of a man who ruled. Cultural interest in this figure is thoroughly ambivalent. The story seems simple: she seduced the enemy, then killed him. She used her sex for deadly purposes. Yet, this is not a story of voyeurism, or of revenge, like that of Tomyris, who is often represented with the head of Cyrus but without an explanation of the reason why

Fig. 6 Massimo Stanzione, *Judith with the Head of Holofernes*,
c. 1630–35, oil on canvas, 199.4 × 146.1 cm (78½ × 57½ in.),
New York, The Metropolitan Museum of Art, Gift of Edward
W. Carter, 1959 (59.40)

she had him killed (pls. 31, 33). Or, to name a blatant victim of voyeurism who did not
triumph so easily—Susanna. She offered ample opportunity for viewers to reiterate the
act of voyeurism. The elders threatened her with death. Viewers in early modern times
didn't need to worry about their guilt, for, in the images, she was already dead (pl. 35).
Carracci's engraving is particularly perverse, as it shows Susanna's breasts frontally,
while also suggesting her complicity with her plight by turning her neck beyond what
seems physically plausible so that she looks the elder in the face. The alibi for this nasty
representation is, of course, narrative: supposedly Susanna is being addressed by the
elder and turns around in surprise. This is another example of the "impurity" of myth.
Similarly, and even less plausible, in plate 31 Tomyris stands naked beside a soldier, and
inspects the head, drawn out of or put into a sack held by a soldier. Her nakedness refers

Fig. 7 Rembrandt van Rijn, *Susanna Surprised by the Elders*, 1647, oil on panel, 76.6 × 92.8 cm (30⅛ × 36½ in.), Berlin, Gemäldegalerie, Staatliche Museen zu Berlin-Preussischer Kulturbesitz, cat. no. 828E

to the scene of voyeurism that took place in her bedroom and for which this murder is the justified revenge. But, visually, we see the sexual body and the danger it/she poses to the men liable to desire her.

Not all representations of victims of voyeurism like Tomyris and Susanna are abusive of course; again, this story is not simple, nor "pure." An Italian painting in this exhibition leaves the figure some dignity (pl. 36). But the principle of representation remains the same: the voyeurs are depicted in the background, plotting together, and the bare-breasted, sexualized Susanna shows her beauty to the viewer, who is thus put into the same position as the voyeurs. Rembrandt's *Susanna* in Berlin makes such a nasty caricature of the spying old men that we can only sympathize with Susanna's plight. Her Venus-like pose is subtly modified to incorporate the gesture of pushing back the threat (fig. 7).

SCHOOL OF THE MUSEUM

Fig. 8 Artemisia Gentileschi, *Judith Beheading Holofernes*, c. 1620, oil on canvas, 199 × 162.5 cm (78¼ × 64 in.), Florence, Uffizi Gallery

Judith, in contrast, is no Tomyris or Susanna, to name two other stories often exploited in order to offer a good look at a naked female body, stories that confirm the official story of women's subjection to the male gaze. The thrill and horror of Judith, as of Delilah and Jael, is that she redefined power itself in terms that bind a conflict of loyalty to access to the sex of the other.

Delilah, for example, appears in series such as Coornhert's after Van Heemskerk, of which there is an example here (pl. 37). Delilah is a good version of the visual "impurity" of the myth. Given her most frequently represented act (cutting Samson's hair while he sleeps), images of Delilah often convey an ambiance of care, a motherliness, which is totally at odds with the "official story" of the murderous seductress (pl. 6). Delilah has Samson between her knees and carefully cuts off his hair. Jael, less frequently represented, can be seen here in the same relentless series by Coornhert (pl. 38).

Delilah's motherly care indicates that something strange happens when the unofficial story gets mixed up with the official one. This mix happens when words and images

Fig. 9 Michelangelo Merisi da Caravaggio, *Judith Beheading Holofernes*, 1598–99, oil on canvas, 145 × 195 cm (57 × 76¾ in.), Rome, Galleria Nazionale d'Arte Antica, Palazzo Barberini

are no longer distinguishable. The two most famous *Judith Beheading Holofernes* paintings in the Western tradition—one by Artemisia Gentileschi, the other by Caravaggio—are perhaps most likely to confront viewers with feelings that neither the literary "source" nor the visual image alone can explain. Feelings such as horror and admiration for a job well done (as in the Gentileschi, fig. 8), or contradictory feelings such as surprise and identification evoked when the face of the decapitated figure turns out to be a self-portrait (as in the Caravaggio, fig. 9). These feelings enhance all the other representations of the Judith theme by foregrounding something that, due to sheer repetition, passes unnoticed too easily. They appeal to the level of emotion, including the contradictions that reign there. Visual images, more easily than literary tales, can absorb contradiction. These images are thereby able to undermine the reiteration of the cultural performance of gender.[9]

These two famous Judith paintings, although allegedly based on the myth, also pervert it. Thus they comment on the phenomenon of myth as social force. In relation to

Fig. 10 Hans Speckaert, *Jael and Sisera*, c. 1576, oil on canvas, 169.5 × 167.5 cm (66¾ × 65⅜ in.), Rotterdam, Museum Boijmans Van Beuningen

that sense of myth, they highlight their own deviations. When deployed and invoked according to the official story, myths such as that of Judith put a frame around women, confining their power to the power of seduction. In that sense the frame is a set-up: women are blamed for their confinement within the Judith role assigned to them. Visual art and imagery are terrifically and terrifyingly efficient tools in the service of such oppressive framing. This raises questions of visual culture: why do certain myths lend themselves for visualization, why are they such attractive subjects, and what do the resulting images do?[10]

The "official story"—the early feminist complaint—would have to opt for a conspiracy theory here: stories end up in images because they serve the propaganda of the dominant gender. But conspiracy theories are naïve and disempowering. I prefer to look at images to see what they reveal about the stories, and vice versa. Stories end up in art, in images, for other reasons as well. They have great dramatic potential. Their combination of beauty and virtue presents a challenge to the subtle painter. Moreover, the story of Judith juxtaposes two loyalties: Judith saves her people but is a threatening figure to men.

In the process of visualizing, some things happen that make it difficult to identify images with the myths they are allegedly "illustrating." In the Judith paintings, there is often an older woman added to the scene (pls. 34, 82). As usual, the older woman, Judith's maid, is important for introducing nuances. In many representations, she is

Fig. 11 Rembrandt van Rijn, *Jael Killing Sisera*, c. 1659–60,
pen and bistre, white body color, 190 × 172 mm (7⅞ × 6¾ in.),
Amsterdam, Rijksmuseum, Rijksprentenkabinet

depicted as a "madame," a procuress, to help establish a contrast that emphasizes the sexuality of the younger woman. This is also why such a female figure is often placed next to Delilah, although the Bible gives no cause for it. In more subtle works, by being contrasted with the older woman, the heroine is depicted as beautiful, attractive—and hence, indirectly, sexual.

The story of Judith is similar to that of Jael killing Sisera, a canonical Old Testament theme found in the books Judges 4 and 5. The Canaanite general Sisera oppresses the people of Israel, after which Barak defeats Sisera's army, and Sisera flees on foot. Jael entices him into her tent and intoxicates him. As he sleeps she drives a tent pin into his temple.[11] Rembrandt's drawing of Jael is an example of a stunningly ambiguous image. According to the iconography, Jael is busy murdering her sleeping victim, but, visually, we see a sculptor making her ideal man, a reversed Pygmalion (fig. 11). We also recognize Delilah's motherly care.

Here, too, a beautiful heroine takes action, saving her people through ruse and sex appeal. In this story, unlike in Judith's, no mention is made of her virtue. In biblical interpretation, this gap has led to a flourish of interpretive leaps—from depicting her as a virtual prostitute to rendering her as a discarded "old hag." Accordingly, painters frame her in ways that fit the theme, that is, in accordance with traditional interpretations of lady-killers. Frequently, we are shown the moment when Jael proudly holds up her prey to Barak, the man in charge, who was unable to achieve the same victory—a double triumph, therefore, of one woman over two men, and, in a certain sense, a mise en scène within the story. In Speckaert's rendering of this myth, her leg is coquettishly displayed, as if to seduce the viewer into believing that this is a story of seduction (fig. 10).

Why is the visual-literary story of the beautiful—or deadly—heroine so popular? Like the different stories of Samson (totally defeated by Delilah because she managed to fiddle the secret of his exceptional powers out of him), and of Jael, that of Judith is one of the popular myths in which the power struggle between men and women ends in favor of "the weak(er) sex." Juxtaposing such myths with historical representations of figures who actually ruled is a strange act indeed: it suggests that women born to rule wrested their power from the men who owned it "naturally," and that they can only have done so by exploiting their sex. To my delight, though, the juxtaposition shows that myths, rather than being opposed to reality, inform it. A king is invested with divine power. A queen can only be naturalized in terms of such sex-based myths, as Judith's story exemplifies. But the binary opposition implied in the antagonistic representations of gender is both reconfirmed and undermined when we acknowledge the second strangeness. For, and even more disturbingly, the frightened imaginings of women who rule stand next to, or opposite, other stories that have also frequently been depicted, in which women are victims of (sexual) violence. We have seen the transition in the figure of Susanna, who withstood voyeurism's subsequent threat of rape and was saved, again, by another man. On the other side of killing women stand the victims. As much as Judith stands for the former category of women, Lucretia stands for the latter. And, bizarrely, these two figures invariably end up in the same collections of images when thematic groupings are at stake.

Lucretia was raped and, to save her—or her husband's—honor, she committed suicide. Susanna (in the Book of Daniel) barely escapes the same fate: she resists the threats of her two attackers, being saved from death by stoning by the young Daniel, who separates the two elders and is thus able to catch them out on their contradictions. Lucretia's presence in collections of women who ruled is another strange aspect. The two strange aspects together—framing women in power as sexual manipulators, and turning victims into their own henchmen—shed unexpected light on the question of if, and how, women can be seen.

The most important aspect of a thematic organization, or frame, thus becomes, for me, the variety of such tensions, not the uniform focus on dangerous women. I submit that this is the key to making this exhibition work: not repeating what one already knows (or thinks one knows), but drawing on other knowledge to increase insight into, on the one hand, more varied relations between the sexes, and, on the other, between individual women and social power. It is a mistake to explain such stories simply as those of victims, of women's wickedness, or of a carnivalesque upside-down world in which women get the upper hand. Instead, they belong, together with the more ambiguous and ambivalent stories, to a series of stories about women, men, and power. This combination of history and genre paintings and prints under the heading of thematics can thus open up the traditional cliché, acknowledging its cultural power and contingency, along with its historical persistence and the possibility of questioning it. From a self-evident and confining frame, thematics can thus become a theoretical frame.

If women's power was conceived as so threatening, ordinary psychology would see in it a projection. In ancient myths, the powerful women who kill somehow seem vengeful, at least in the reception of their stories, to which the images in this exhibition bear witness. It is not hard to imagine the possibility that women might well be compelled to kill men as a reaction to the killing of women, which is much more frequent. Far from being a mistake, Lucretia's presence thus betrays the double issue of projection from guilt, and of making hypervisible what the male look cannot bear to see.[12]

In fact I submit that these two aspects are causally connected. If men are so frightened to see femininity in the face that they must destroy what seduces them, then turning the killed into the killer makes all the sense in the world. If, in historical reality, women actually end up in power positions, the psycho-cultural mechanism of projection comes in handy. The knot of these unreflected—but not necessarily always unconscious!—mechanisms would produce such a messy, inextricable combination of often narratively shaped complexes that it seems appealing to see in it a source of the desire to mess up neat categories in general. I will now try to unravel a few of these strands through Lucretia's presence.

A WAR OF IMAGES

The Lucretia story, which came to us through the Latin classical canon, from Livy and Ovid, has been recycled many times throughout the history of Western literature: church fathers, medieval allegories, and Renaissance poetry and painting were all fond of it for

Fig. 12 Rembrandt van Rijn, *Lucretia*, 1664, oil on canvas, 120 × 101 cm (47¼ × 39¾ in.), National Gallery of Art, Washington, Andrew W. Mellon Collection

the opportunity it offered of fine-tuning juridical and theological questions of the right-to-life versus the right-to-choice. It made it into opera and theater. Numerous works of art exploited the opportunity it presented to whitewash the nude with moral righteousness, such as the engraving by Marcantonio Raimondi, who clearly refers to the classical, heroic source story (pl. 39).

I remember when I first saw Rembrandt's 1664 *Lucretia*, in the National Gallery of Art in Washington, D.C. (fig. 12). I saw it obliquely, from the right, and suddenly. The painting was in the conservation studio, covered by a cloth that was quickly removed. I was standing on the right side of the easel when it was uncovered. This position together with the suddenness determined what I saw. As a result of that random viewing moment, before anything else I saw movement. The figure moved her head, away from me. Later I realized this strong sense of movement was produced by the tiniest of details: the fact that the earring in Lucretia's left ear doesn't hang straight. As a result, it is as if she is swinging her head away from the viewer. Reading the earlier painting, narratively, "for the plot," we would interpret Lucretia's movement as a consequence of the presence of the men. Father and husband are trying to comfort her when suddenly she kills herself, for she has to act swiftly before they restrain her.

Such a reading emerges from the narrativity effect triggered by the earring.[13] It takes the motivations from the story, projecting the latter onto the scene as it is depicted. It is also verbal in the traditional sense, since it superimposes on the painting an "underlying" verbal story, which the painting is then supposed to "illustrate." The appeal to such a realistic reading demonstrates the extent to which art and its interpretation depend on the relations between visual and verbal texts, in both directions. To account for this "impurity," I propose a concept of "visual verbality," in which rhetoric, a representational strategy traditionally associated with verbal communication, is conceived in visual terms. As a consequence, the relationship between images and verbal sources must be conceived of in a radically different way—not as offering two layers of meaning but as providing an intricate interaction.

The Lucretia theme theorizes what is at stake in "showing," including in this exhibition on images of women in power. For me "exposition" became programmatic for cultural analysis. In my book *Double Exposures*, I tried to connect three terms deriving from the verb "to expose": exposition, exposé, and exposure. These are the three issues a cultural analysis of visual imagery brings together. The verb refers to "making a public presentation" or "demonstrating publicly"; as a noun it can mean opinions or judgments and refer to the public presentation of someone's views; and it can refer to the performing of those deeds that deserve to be made public.

Some aspect or version of each of these meanings is central to the issues I see as the agenda for cultural analysis "beyond"—after, as well as in continuation of—the disciplinary humanities. To make the point right away: the triple meaning of the verb "to expose" in this sense constitutes the field of cultural analysis because it defines cultural behavior, if not "culture" as such. This is why the Lucretia story is not an exception in this exhibition, but its core. It has visual description as its primary agent, as its murderer. From time immemorial, the name "Lucretia" has signified a narrative of triple victimization: this Roman heroine was raped; then she killed herself, unable to judge in favor of life once her subjectivity had been effectively destroyed; and, finally, her story was erased by the tradition of rhetorical reading that interpreted it, ironically, as "just" an allegory of the victory of democracy over tyranny.

The rape of Lucretia is, indeed, a war of images. Two of the most powerful and effective visual representations of Lucretia, those by Rembrandt, are also profoundly rhetorical. Two years after painting the *Lucretia* now found in Washington, Rembrandt painted another one, currently located in the Minneapolis Institute of Arts (fig. 13). Whereas the Washington *Lucretia* shows the figure when she is about to stab herself, the other shows her immediately after the stabbing, with a bloody wound and with her hand at the bell rope to call her witnesses. Those witnesses, her husband and her father, are rarely depicted, although we do see such a classical witness figure, reminiscent of the chorus in Greek tragedy, depicted in a woodcut by Moreelse in this exhibition (pl. 40). Clearly, the wound stands as a metaphor for the body part that was attacked. As I have argued elsewhere, rhetoric constructs reality through the construction of the meanings it offers reality to work with. That is to say, the rhetorical analysis does not stand in

Fig. 13 Rembrandt van Rijn, *Lucretia*, 1666, oil on canvas, 105.1 × 92.3 cm (41⅜ × 36⅜ in.), Minneapolis, The Minneapolis Institute of Arts

opposition to the real issue of rape. Rather, it partakes of it, with the rhetorical figurations helping both to construct the views of rape dominant in the culture in which the rhetorical discourse or image functions and to condition responses to real rape.

The importance of seriously attending to rhetoric becomes obvious as soon as we look again at the metaphor of suicide in the Rembrandt. The use of metaphor raises the question of motivation: why compare the content of the metaphor with this metaphoric image? This motivation is more often than not metonymical: a sign represents the rape, not by similitude but by temporal contiguity, and, as a consequence, a sign can represent its cause, or a later event its predecessor. Read metonymically, then, we would interpret the scene depicted in the *Lucretia* paintings as follows: rape is like self-murder (metaphor) because rape leads to self-murder (metonymy). In other words, the choice of a rhetorical term is itself an ideological decision. By limiting ourselves to metaphor, we displace responsibility onto the victim—emphasizing "self" rather than "murder." In contrast, if we use metonymy as well, responsibility is returned to where it belongs: to the rapist and the rape as destruction—to murder rather than to "self."

Synecdoche, taking the detail to stand for the whole—pars pro toto—can become another important tool for reading the painting. By using this rhetorical strategy, self-murder becomes the "detail" representing the entire process. Lucretia's raped body-part comes to stand for her whole person, just as her suicide, her act that stands for herself, comes to stand for the entire story—the rape-and-its-consequence. Not only is the rape itself thus brought back into sight, but it recovers its place as the act that brings about the murder of the self.

Hence, this odd case of an utterly disempowered woman in a display of "women who ruled" contributes in important ways to undermining the various essentialisms involved in a flatly thematic, "purely" visual, artistic and fictionalizing, thematic exhibition.

THE POWER OF (IN)VISIBILITY

With Judith on the one hand and Lucretia on the other, it is tempting to look back again at the portraits of Queen Elizabeth and other figures like her—Anne of Austria, Marie de' Medici and Christina of Sweden, all women who "really" ruled. The nearly obsessive effort in the portraits of Elizabeth to highlight her face (a rather dead face at that), as if to underscore the invisibility of her body, now becomes extremely meaningful—and painful (figs. 14, 15). Perhaps, as Julia Kristeva hinted, there is a murderous quality to the portrait as genre.[14] The portrait is a visual case of beheading. Not a cause: it is not because women are abused and exploited by voyeurism that they set out to vengefully behead men; but a case: by representing the face, so difficult to read for the tortured Lucretia, the painter performs a beheading.

The reason? Look at the nude. Then, look again at the Queen. If the nude is a case of objectification, of the killing gaze, one of Lucas Cranach the Elder's many *Lucretia* paintings does a terrific job at it (fig. 17). Her attempt at chastity is stolen from her; the veil meant to cover her is mercilessly transparent. But her assaulted body looks dead already. It is only a still shape. Her face is not distinguishable from that of Salome

Fig. 14 Nicholas Hilliard, *Portrait of Queen Elizabeth I*, c. 1595–1600, oil on vellum, 54 × 45 mm (2⅛ × 1¾ in.), Montreal, Montreal Museum of Fine Arts, Gift of Mrs. F. Cleveland Morgan.

(fig. 18) and Judith (fig. 16), those two colleagues in sex crime. So, if representing the female body is a way of killing her, it makes no difference whether "woman" is put on display as nude or as face-only. Either way, the live creature, a woman—not one who rules but one who just lives—cannot be imagined in a culture of misogyny. Her existence must be turned into a case, encased, flattened—in any of the ways visual culture has at its disposal—so that she can remain invisible. The hypervisibility of women in power is only another way of killing them.

Fig. 15 Anonymous (Britain), *Elizabeth I, Queen of England*, c. 1588, oil on canvas, 76.2 × 63.5 cm (30 × 25 in.), Toledo, Toledo Museum of Art; Purchased with funds from the Libbey Endowment, Gift of Edward Drummond Libbey; acc. no. 1953.94

Fig. 16 Lucas Cranach the Elder, *Judith*, c. 1530, oil on limewood panel, 86 × 59 cm (33⅞ × 23¼ in.), Stuttgart, Staatsgalerie Stuttgart

Fig. 17 Lucas Cranach the Elder, *Lucretia*,
1533, oil on panel, 37.3 × 23.9 cm
(14 × 9 in.), Berlin, Gemäldegalerie,
Staatliche Museen zu Berlin-Preussischer
Kulturbesitz, cat. no. 1832

Fig. 18 Lucas Cranach the Elder, *The Feast of Herod*, 1531, oil on panel, 81.3 × 119.8 cm (32 × 47⅛ in.), Hartford, Wadsworth Atheneum, The Ella Gallup Sumner and Mary Catlin Sumner Collection Fund, 1936.339

NOTES

1   On the political function of the representation of royal figures, Louis Marin's study (1981) offers brilliant insights. He argues that representation transforms the potential force and violence of royal power twice, first transforming violence into power, then justifying that power as legitimate and necessary.

2   On the contest for beauty and the inevitable place of sexuality in such fantasies, see Damisch 1992.

3   On the visual fascination of the figure of Medusa and its background in an anthropology of vision, see Clair 1989.

4   The paradigmatic essay is Laura Mulvey's still unforgotten 1975 article, "Visual Pleasure and Narrative Cinema" (Mulvey 1975). Within a psychoanalytic argument the school to which Mulvey's essay belonged claimed that castration anxiety made looking at female bodies a daring, dangerous, and necessary apprenticeship of masculinity. As a consequence, all cultural effort went into representing women as passive objects exposed for the voyeuristic male gaze.

5   Rosenberg 1970–71, p. 24, figs. 9–10.

6   I argued for a reconsideration of the notion of myth in view of visual representations that never quite match the stories they purportedly illustrate; see Bal 1991.

7   I have discussed the complexities of the Judith myth in Bal 1995.

8   For a discussion of this work, see Jacobus 1986.

9   I use this formulation to invoke Judith Butler's theory (1993) according to which sex and gender are not "natural" but culturally learned, through a reiterative imitation or "citation" of roles culturally performed.

10 I use the term "framing" here in the sense of both "set-up" and "context." For a clear and concise formulation, see the Author's Preface to Culler 1988.

11 See Bal (1988b) on this story and its implications for the methodology of interdisciplinary study.

12 I have suggested this projection theory of killing women *à propos* of the Book of Judges, where three stories of each—men killing innocent young women and (older, more mature, perhaps motherly) women killing men— suggest such a theory quite strongly; see Bal, 1988a.

13 On this effect and Rembrandt's two *Lucretia* paintings, see chap. 2 of my book *Reading "Rembrandt"* (Bal 1991).

14 *Visions capitales*, 1998.

24

ANONYMOUS
German, 17th century
Judith, Venus, and
Lucretia, tankard with
cover

1639
Silver, partially gilded, repoussé and
engraved
Height 143 × width 130 × diam.
101 mm (height 5⅝ × width 5⅛ ×
diam. 4 in.) including handle
Ann Arbor, University of Michigan
Museum of Art, 1966

The three raised silver gilt
medallions on this tankard depict
scenes of Judith, Lucretia, and
Venus—all shown nude. While
Judith and Lucretia figured in
famous women series
(combining figures from
antiquity, figures from the Old
Testament, and Christian women
from the remote or recent past),
the figure of Venus is anomalous.
Each figure seems to suggest a
different role in stories of
seduction: dominatrix (Judith),
victim (Lucretia), and inspirer of
love (Venus). Silver objects such
as this tankard were often given
as courtship or wedding gifts.

HENDRICK GOLTZIUS
Dutch, 1558–1617
Helen of Troy

1615
Oil on canvas
115 × 83.3 cm (45¼ × 32¾ in.)
Lent in honor of Professor Emeritus
Charles Sawyer by a former pupil

Helen of Troy was the famous
beauty of Homer's *Iliad*, whose
abduction by Paris, the prince
of Troy, touched off the Trojan
War. The apple lying on the table
before her alludes to the story of
the Judgment of Paris, in which
Venus induces Paris to fall in love
with Helen. This unusual,
portrait-like image of Helen
seems an invitation to admire
her beauty, the shimmering
colors of her costume playing
off the tones of her skin and
hair, but also to meditate on the
dangerous power of a woman's
beauty.

Simon Vouet
French, 1590–1649
The Toilette of Venus

c. 1640–45
Oil on canvas
165 × 115 cm (65 × 45¼ in.)
Pittsburgh, Carnegie Museum of Art,
Gift of Mrs. Horace Binney Hare,
1952

In Vouet's *Toilette of Venus*, Venus assumes a classical pose of modesty, covering up before our gaze as we have caught her in what seems to be a private moment in her boudoir. As our eyes meet hers in the mirror, however, it becomes unclear who is caught off guard, and which party in this game of gazes is really in control. Yet alongside Venus's knowing look, her gesture appears to be more seductive than truly modest. It is in the mirror that the painting's ambiguity seems concentrated: desire, vanity, and deception are all suggested by its reflective surface.

27

JEROME WIERIX
Flemish, c. 1553–1619
After HANS SEBALD
BEHAM
German, 1500–1550
*Judith Walking to the
Left, and Her Servant*

1613
Engraving
115 × 73 mm (4½ × 2⅞ in.)
Albion, The Albion College
Permanent Print Collection

The nudity of the heroine in this
print by Wierix (after Beham)
would seem at first glance to
emphasize Judith's seductiveness.
This is offset, however, by other
elements in the image: Judith's
striding stance, which suggests a
more active power, and her firm
grip on the sizeable sword. The
intertwined bodies of Judith and
her maid also stress their
conspiratorial relationship in the
effort to bring down Holofernes.

28

DIRCK VOLKERTSZ.
COORNHERT
Dutch, 1522–1590
After MAARTEN VAN
HEEMSKERCK
Dutch, 1498–1574
*Judith Slaying
Holofernes, from
The Power of Women,
a set of six*

1551
Engraving and etching
248 × 194 mm (9¾ × 7⅝ in.)
Lent by The Metropolitan Museum
of Art, New York, Rogers Fund,
1966

Dirck Volkertsz. Coornhert
worked in Haarlem as the
principal engraver of Maarten
van Heemskerck. Their
collaboration produced a series
of six images on the misogynist
power of women theme. Here
Eve, Lot's daughters, Jael,
Delilah, Judith, and the Queen
of Sheba are represented as
strong, muscular females. Their
androgyny and the violence of
their actions vividly
communicate their danger.

.23.

Hic ubi fœda rubent cóſperſa conopéa tabo
Obrute fœminea Ductor ab arte iaces.

OLOFERNES OCCIDI-
TVR.

Exitio forma illa tuo ſe compſcrat at tu
Noxturnam properas ebrietate necem.

29

ANTONIO TEMPESTA
Italian, 1555–1630
Judith and Holofernes,
from Biblical Battles

1613
Etching
206 × 284 mm (8⅛ × 11⅛ in.)
plate
Cambridge, Fogg Art Museum,
Harvard University Art Museums,
Gift of Melvin R. Seiden

One of twenty-four etchings in
Tempesta's Biblical Battles series,
which was dedicated to Cosimo
de' Medici II, the Grand Duke
of Florence, this scene alone
features a female protagonist.
It is tempting to think that this
might be connected to the special
significance Judith had to the
Medici and to Florence. It is
somewhat rare to find Judith
represented in a battlefield.
Setting Judith in this context
perhaps suggests that her act be
viewed as one of military valor.

30

ELISABETTA SIRANI
Italian, 1638–1665
Judith

c. 1662
Oil on canvas
124.5 × 162.8 cm (49 × 64 in.)
University Art Museum, University
of California, Santa Barbara, Gift of
Gary C. Gallup

This painting showing the biblical heroine Judith with her handmaiden is tantalizing in that it is difficult to know precisely which moment of the story is depicted. It could show the women as they prepare to enter general Holofernes's tent for the feast at which Judith will seduce and kill him. Or it could represent both women on their way back to their homeland, Bethulia. Judith pauses, perhaps as she ponders her divinely ordained duty—either before carrying out her deed, or in its aftermath. The draped trumpet alludes to Judith's victory to come or its successful accomplishment.

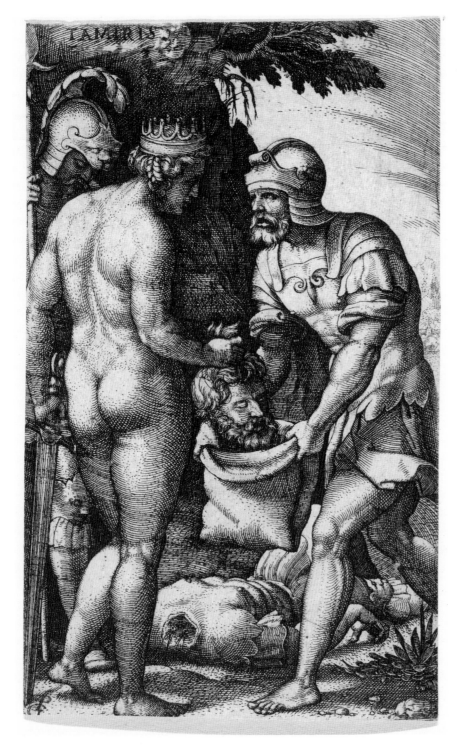

31
GEORG PENCZ
German, c. 1500–1550

Tomyris with the Head of Cyrus

c. 1539
Engraving
117 × 73 mm (4¾ × 2⅞ in.) sheet
Cambridge, Fogg Art Museum,
Harvard University Art Museums,
Gift of William Gray from the
collection of Francis Calley Gray

Tomyris was the legendary
queen of the Massagetae who
plunged the decapitated head
of King Cyrus of Persia into a
bucket of blood in revenge for
her son's death. While Tomyris
is presented as an honorable
woman and ruler by Herodotus,
Pencz has veered from the text,
rendering her as a nude
seductress. The engraving seems
to suggest that Tomyris defeated
Cyrus with her feminine wiles,
rather than with her intelligence
as a ruler.

32
FEDE GALIZIA
Italian, c. 1578–1630

Judith with the Head of Holofernes

1596
Oil on canvas
120.5 × 94 cm (47½ × 37 in.)
Gift of Mr. and Mrs. Jacob Polak,
The John and Mable Ringling
Museum of Art, Sarasota

This painting of Judith with the
head of Holofernes is by the
female painter Fede Galizia, who
became famous in Milan as a
portrait painter. Judith's
elaborate costume and lavish
jewelry stress her comeliness,
while her alert, purposeful
attitude emphasizes her heroism.
With the artist's name and the
date of the painting inscribed on
the sword blade, this traditional
masculine weapon becomes a
testimony of the prowess of the
artist herself.

SATIA TE SANGVINE QVEM SEMPER SITISTI.

33

PAULUS PONTIUS
Flemish, 1603–1658
After PETER PAUL
RUBENS
Flemish, 1577–1640
The Head of Cyrus
Brought to Queen
Tomyris

1630
Engraving
403 × 588 mm
(15⅞ × 23⅛ in.) plate,
410 × 515 mm
(16⅛ × 23½ in.) sheet
Lent by the Museum of Fine Arts,
Boston, Stephen Bullard Memorial
Fund

Pontius's print, after an important
painting by Rubens, now at the
Boston Museum of Fine Arts,
represents the story of Queen
Tomyris and Cyrus at the
moment that Tomyris's pledge of
revenge for the death of her son
is fulfilled. Tomyris had promised
to give Cyrus, the bloodthirsty
king of Persia, his fill of blood,
and thus she has his decapitated
head submerged in blood. The
small dog lapping at the blood,
a detail not found in Rubens's
painting, stresses the cruel justice
of the event. Tomyris' costume,
her elevated position on a dais,
and her appearance amid her full
court signal her importance.

34

GIOVANNI BATTISTA
DI JACOPO, called
ROSSO FIORENTINO
Italian, 1494–1540
Judith with the Head
of Holofernes

c. 1535–40
Red chalk
232 × 197 mm (9⅛ x 7¾ in.)
Los Angeles, Los Angeles County
Museum of Art, Dalzell Hatfield
Memorial Fund

Rosso's startling drawing
transforms the story of Judith
into a vanitas theme, a
meditation on the inevitable
passing of all things. By
portraying Judith nude, it
strongly suggests that it was
solely due to her beauty and
sexual allure that she was able to
conquer Holofernes. At the same
time, the juxtaposition of
Judith's youthful body with the
wizened body of her maid
implies the transience of this
beauty, and thus the fleeting
nature of women's power.

35

ANNIBALE CARRACCI
Italian, 1560–1609

Susanna and the Elders

1590
Etching and engraving
333 × 310 mm
(13⅛ × 12¼ in.)
Ann Arbor, University of Michigan
Museum of Art, 1959

Like many representations of
Susanna and the elders, Carracci's
widely circulated print departs
from the biblical text in its
sensualization of the subject.
Susanna bathes in a lush garden,
the fountain before her
decorated with symbols of love
and desire. Although she appears
to pull away from the pleading
gesticulations of the elders, her
expression seems to indicate
amused pleasure at the power of
her charms. Her partial covering
of herself enhances the scene's
eroticism. Susanna's pose is
modeled after the crouching
Venus, which in itself carries
erotic connotations.

36

MASSIMO STANZIONE
Italian, 1585–1656
Susanna and the Elders

1631–37
Oil on canvas
158 × 178.6 cm (60 × 70¼ in.)
Joslyn Art Museum, Omaha,
Museum purchase

Stanzione's painting of Susanna poses a notable contrast to most sixteenth- and seventeenth-century depictions of the subject, which commonly eroticize the story, and sometimes even suggest a willingness on Susanna's part in her violation. Susanna appears as a formidable, even monumental figure in the foreground. Gripping her drapery at her ankle, she endeavors to keep her lower body concealed as she bathes, and the nudity of her upper body seems less sexual than heroic. Instead of encouraging the viewer to join the elders (the conspiring interlopers in the background) in their voyeurism, the painting fosters a sympathy with the virtuous Susanna.

37

DIRCK VOLKERTSZ.
COORNHERT
Dutch, 1522–1590
After MAARTEN VAN
HEEMSKERCK
Dutch, 1498–1574
*Samson and Delilah,
from The Power of
Women, a set of six*
1551
Engraving and etching
248 × 197 mm (9¾ × 7¾ in.)
Lent by The Metropolitan Museum
of Art, New York, Rogers Fund,
1966

38
DIRCK VOLKERTSZ.
COORNHERT
Dutch, 1522–1590
After MAARTEN VAN
HEEMSKERCK
Dutch, 1498–1574
Jael Slaying Sisera, from
The Power of Women,
a set of six

1551
Engraving and etching
250 × 195 mm (9⅞ × 7⅝ in.)
Lent by The Metropolitan Museum
of Art, New York, Rogers Fund,
1966

AMEINON
ANOΘNHCKEIN
N,
H AICXPῶC,
ZHN

39
MARCANTONIO
RAIMONDI
Italian, 1480–1527/34
After RAPHAEL
Italian, 1483–1520
Death of Lucretia

c. 1511–12
Engraving
214 × 134 mm (8½ × 5¼ in.)
sheet, trimmed on platemark
Lent by the Museum of Fine Arts,
Boston, Gift of Mrs. T. Jefferson
Coolidge

Marcantonio's engraving, based
on a drawing by Raphael, was
one of the best-known images of
Lucretia in the Renaissance. The
classical basis of Lucretia's pose
accords the figure a heroic
nobility, while the bare breast
and bunching of drapery at her
pubic area eroticize the figure.

40

PAULUS MOREELSE
Dutch, 1571–1638
Death of Lucretia

1612
Woodcut
257 × 329 mm (10⅛ × 13 in.)
Ann Arbor, University of Michigan
Museum of Art, 1959

Moreelse's woodcut shows the
Roman heroine Lucretia just
after she has committed suicide.
Her elderly maidservant's
outstretched hands express
horror at the tragedy of her
death. Lucretia was held up to
Renaissance women as a model
of chastity and obedience to
patriarchal values. Following her
rape by Sextus Tarquinius, the
son of the Etruscan king, she
denounced him to her father and
husband so as to establish her
innocence. Her kinsmen sought
revenge by overthrowing the
Etruscans and establishing the
Roman Republic.

Is the King Genderless? The Staging of the Female Regent as Minerva Pacifera

BETTINA BAUMGÄRTEL

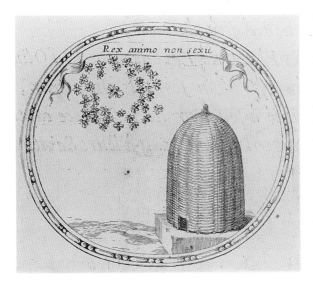

Fig. 19 Anonymous, *Rex animo non sexu*, emblem in Pierre Le Moyne, *La Gallerie des femmes fortes*, Paris, Chez Antoine de Sommaville, 1647, engraving and etching, 83 × 97 mm (3¼ × 3⅞ in.), New Haven, The Beinecke Rare Book and Manuscript Library, Yale University

Opposite: Gerrit van Honthorst, *Artemisia*, 1632–1635 (pl. 43, detail)

The introduction to Pierre Le Moyne's work *La Gallerie des femmes fortes*, dedicated to the French regent Anne of Austria, displays an emblem with the motto "*Rex animo non sexu*," maintaining that spirit, not gender, defines a king (fig. 19). This moral imperative, that the highest office in the state be occupied regardless of gender and according to spiritual greatness, has different origins: for one, the theory of the king's two bodies seems to bear an influence here. As Ernst H. Kantorowicz explains, the modern state that was born out of early medieval political theology constructed a new state theory whereby church doctrine was transformed into the two bodies legal doctrine.[1] The duality of king and law now replaced the former duality of Christ (religious ruler) and king (secular ruler). The English judges of the Tudor period substantiated this distinction between the *body politic* and the *body natural* not least of all to secure the line of succession after the death of the king. Thus, over time, the notion of the king's supernatural, immortal body, cleansed of all the imperfections, sins, and frailties of the natural body, developed. Age, such as the underage status of the heir apparent, had no effect upon the competency of the body politic. The body of the state, symbolized by the crown, does not die—*corona non moritur*—but continues to live on in the heir to the throne. The body of the state, described as a "*character angelus*" (angelic character), also does not seem bound to gender. One could assume that the two bodies theory, a construct obviously based on gender equality, would not exclude the female gender.

In practice, however, the application of the principles of civil law and the law of inheritance to national law prevented the equal treatment of the female regent. Marital law followed the principle, already formulated in the Bible, that the husband was head of the wife and the wife was the body of the husband (Eph. 5). Comparable laws about the relationship between a ruler and subject were derived from these rights of a husband over his wife. Marital law stipulated, among other things, that while the husband could make use of his wife's possessions, he could not sell them. In order to protect fiscal property, its inalienability was explained in terms of this principle of private law.[2] The doctrine of the political body may have been based on gender equality; in the modern state, however, a patriarchal theology in secular form continued that was tied to the royal priesthood and the ruler as God's representative on earth.

In this context, one should mention a clever strategy that was employed by some of the female regents. In order to make the figure of the queen on the throne plausible as

God's representative, which the state had not yet accepted for the queen mother, they invoked the church's enforced enthronement of the Mother of God next to God the Father and God the Son. Anne of Austria's dual strategy becomes apparent when she lets her predecessor Blanche of Castile be depicted in the guise of the Virgin Mary, sitting on the celestial throne as the personification of religion (fig. 20). In her predecessor, the queen mother, the country's two highest powers, church and state, are united into one sacrosanct office that transcends time. Her devoutness, a virtue identified as a specifically female strength in the work of the *Querelle des femmes*, is not only one of the four Christian cardinal virtues, but is also elevated here to the highest ruler's virtue. The particular aptitude of women to assume governmental office is suggested in this disguised visual message that appeals to the figure of the Mother of God.[3]

The application of private inheritance law to the context of national law led to a patriarchal line of succession from father to son that disadvantaged female descendants. If the king and heir to the throne are understood as an inseparable unity in a line of succession, then a deputy interregnum is at best all that remains for the female ruler.

Since the fourteenth century, under Salic law in France, female rulers were constitutionally barred from ascending to the throne, but could act as regents. Consequently, clever strategies were devised to circumvent the centuries-old law of succession and to constructively utilize the idea of the king's immortal political body to preserve one's own power. Even if, on a purely legal basis, Catherine de' Medici, Marie de' Medici, and Anne of Austria only became regents in the absence of the king or as substitutes for their underage sons, their reigns in practice corresponded, for the most part, to the fully sovereign rule of a king. In order to legitimize and solidify their legally insecure position afterward, they propagated a canon of virtues specifically suited to the situation of female reign. As proof of their ability to rule, they defied the widely disseminated prejudice that women were uneducable and sinful, demonstrating wisdom and virtue, as well as a skillful hand in government affairs, bringing affluence and peace. In this regard, the figure of Minerva served as the ideal embodiment of this political message.

BLANCHE DE CASTILLE.
En l'habit de Religion qu'elle prit peu auant sa mort.

Fig. 20 Grégoire Huret, *Blanche of Castile as Religion* in Charles Combault d'Auteuil, *Blanche infante de Castille, mère de Saint Louis*, Paris, Chez Antoine de Sommaville ... et Augustin Courbé ..., 1644, engraving, 230 × 155 mm (9 × 6⅛ in.), Paris, Bibliothèque nationale de France, N2

ARTEMISIA AS INCORPORATION OF THE KING'S BODY POLITIC

At the same time, a widow's iconography developed in response to the specific situation of a queen widow. Artemisia and other historical, mythical, or biblical models (such as Sophonisba, Lucretia, or Esther) played a central role as symbols of absolute marital fidelity or chastity beyond the death of one's spouse. As Barbara Gaehtgens points out, the figure of Artemisia as widow, who swallowed her deceased husband's ashes, became particularly relevant during the reign of Catherine de' Medici.[4] The act of drinking ashes was to symbolize the incorporation of the king's power (pls. 42, 43). In contradiction to Gaehtgens's arguments, it seems to me that the widow's iconography falls short, however, in its attempt to make manifest the complete transformation of the female regent's body natural into a functional body politic. The figure of Artemisia and corresponding widow's ethic is by no means an equivalent to the ruler's iconography. The act of drinking the ashes does not symbolize the transformation of the royal body, but rather the incorporation or absorption of the king's body politic into a substituting body. The king's body is and remains the symbol of state power. The body of the female regent is only a container or shell for the king's power, both in terms of her function as widow and "burial site" for her husband's ashes and as stand-in for the not yet matured body politic of her son. As such, the body of the regent is never the actual; it is always merely a signifier of male power and never an expression of itself, that is, an expression of legitimate female power.

The French female regent was also unable to carry out the division of the king's two bodies, described by Kantorowicz, with her specific widow's iconography for the very reason that her role as a widow placed her in a gendered role as wife and mother. In the end, the regent's body natural continues to remain visible in the figure of Artemisia and the associated widow's ethic with specifically feminine connotations, so that no body politic can be constituted independent of it. Her strategy therefore entails reinterpreting and re-evaluating this gendered role as a political purpose that transcends gender. In this respect, it is only consistent that an ambivalence in the allegorical state portrait of the regent be sought that could suggest alternating associations with the natural, female body, as well as the official, political role. In the case of the regent, therefore, a clear separation between the body politic and the body natural did not take place, but rather a mixing and overlapping of the feminine into the political.

Marie de' Medici, in particular, was a master of this dual strategy. On February 26, 1622, Peter Paul Rubens signed a contract regarding the production of two painting cycles. The upper floor of the west wing in the Luxembourg Palace was to be decorated with paintings about the history of the queen, the east wing with paintings about the history of Henri IV. Only the Medici cycle was completed. Today the twenty-six paintings in large format are located in the Louvre.

The Medici cycle is a revealing example of the consistent politicization of her feminine roles as candidate for marriage, wife, and queen mother, thereby revealing the possibility of dual association of a *natural*, feminine regent's body and a *political* body functioning as the bearer of the king's power. The cycle shows that the figure of Minerva, who still counts as an example of gender-crossing today—that is, she is referred to in terms of role reversal and the masculinization of women—became the female equivalent of Hercules and an official, political metaphor for feminine power and wisdom.

THE EQUALITY OF DIFFERENCE OF THE SEXES

The Le Moynean motto is said to stem from the reservoir of arguments used in the Querelle des femmes that had been ongoing since the beginnings of the modern age.[5] If mental ability, regardless of gender, determines whether a man or a woman ascends to the throne, this presupposes that the woman has the same mental abilities as the man. The motto is thereby based upon the belief in the equality of the sexes. A liberating eschatological doctrine underlies this belief, wherein all gender differences cancel each other out in the ideal of humanity as undifferentiated by gender.

In its undiminished form, Aristotelian-scholastic philosophy provided a model for the doctrine of equality, as well as the doctrine of the two bodies. According to this philosophy, sexuality is of importance for the mere purpose of procreation, whereas the significance of the body is only accidental. Mind and soul, on the other hand, strive to attain a higher goal, the perfection of humanity as a unity undifferentiated by gender.[6]

Marie de Gournay (1565–1645), the founder of French feminism, can be seen as the quick-to-learn successor of the Aristotelian body of thought. In her pioneering 1622 polemic L'Egalité des hommes et des femmes, purposefully dedicated to the regent Anne of Austria, she skillfully employed Aristotelian argumentation to exclude, from the very onset, the debate concerning the superiority or inferiority of one sex over the other. "If one takes it seriously," she wrote, "a human being is neither a man nor a woman. The opposite sex is not there to elaborate a difference in the human species, but merely to serve as a means of procreation. The possession of a rational soul is its only significant trait. If one might make a little joke, then the following suggestive remark would be fitting: nothing resembles the tomcat sitting on a windowsill more than—the cat."[7]

This argument possibly fell on fertile ground with Anne of Austria so that Pierre Le Moyne, following Marie de Gournay, could rest assured that the regent would receive his motto "Rex animo non sexu" in good will. Interestingly, however, the emblem's pictorial message and the motto have divergent goals. The image shows a queen bee surrounded by a swarm of bees next to a beehive. This reference to the animal world not only proves that women can rule a state as well as men can, but more importantly, by focusing on female supremacy in the bee colony, it suggests the superiority of female reign.[8] The bee colony represents a well-organized and exemplary state, in which the subordination of the man to the queen's right of disposal is considered part of a functioning system. On the surface, image and text seem to complement one another. Considered more closely, however, they give opposite messages. Gender equality, or rather, the lack of difference between the sexes postulated in the text is contradicted by the image that suggests the superiority of the female sex and thereby gender differences.

Significant political events in Europe during the mid-sixteenth to mid-seventeenth century played a role in rekindling the debate about the equality of women. Elizabeth I first ascended to the English throne in 1558 after the parliamentary attempt to exclude her from the line of succession failed. Two years later, Catherine de' Medici came to the French throne after the death of Henri II and the brief reign of her son, Francis II. When Marie de' Medici was crowned as French queen in Saint Denis on May 13, 1610, and on the next day Henri IV was assassinated by Catholic fanatics, the queen widow took over the regency for her underage son Louis XIII (pl. 46). When, in turn, he died in 1643, his widow, Anne of Austria, ruled in the place of her underage son Louis XIV until 1661. Many powerful women from the high nobility participated in politics during her reign. Anne-Geneviève of Bourbon, the duchess of Longueville (1619–1679) joined in as one of the early factionists in the uprising of the nobility. In the year 1648, the faction joined the parliament in standing up against the Crown, represented by Anne of Austria. Anne Marie Louise of Orléans, known as La Grande Mademoiselle (1627–1693), daughter of Louis XIII's younger brother, was another influential representative of the high nobility. In her native town of Orléans in 1652, she took part in the struggle of the nobility against the kingship as an Amazon-like heroine. Two years earlier, in 1650, another "amazon," Christina of Sweden, was elevated to the throne.

Fig. 21 Abraham Bosse, *Louis XIII as the Gallic Hercules*, 1635, engraving, 285 × 345 mm (11¼ × 13⅝ in.), Paris, Bibliothèque nationale de France

"La soif de régnier"—RULING IS A NOBLER PASSION THAN LOVE

The debate about whether women are capable of assuming power and ruling successfully is mirrored in the body of work that was commissioned not only by the regents themselves and those within the court, but also by those in opposition to the court. Numerous pictorial cycles, such as that illustrating Pierre Le Moyne's *La Gallerie des Femmes Fortes*, extol the heroism of women without losing sight of the goal to redirect women's responsibility for public welfare into the domestic domain and to reintroduce the old moral code of chastity and modesty through the back door.[9] At the same time, misogynist pamphlets and so-called *"Weiberlisten"* (Women's ruses) warned against the pernicious power of women.[10] The mythological subject of Hercules and Omphale was among the established repertoire of serial works about powerful women. The strong hero was a slave to the Lydian queen Omphale for three years and consented to a role reversal.

If, according to the Luxembourg Palace inventory, Marie de' Medici had the painting *Hercules and Omphale* by Simon Vouet, now lost, hung over her mantelpiece in 1639 (pl. 44), one can assume that the previously negative connotation of the subject matter had undergone a change in meaning.[11] It is highly unlikely that Marie de' Medici would have used the subject in the traditional fashion as a satire of marriage or as a mockery of the "topsy-turvy world," wherein female rule was depicted as unjust and unnatural. Rather, the distich of the reproduced work references a different conceptual plane. The figure of Cupid, who is aiming at Hercules, invites us to read the painting as an expression of the loss of strength through love. In the context of the queen's chamber, the warning is directed first and foremost at the *femme forte*, that is, at the regent herself. If she eludes the power of love, she remains able to rule. Under this premise, the common interpretation of Omphale as signifying sensual pleasure or as an example of the abuse of power could be set aside.

The significance of Hercules should also be considered anew here. As twin figure between God and man, he ideally corresponds to the concept of the king's dual body.[12] He dedicated his life and deeds to the welfare of humanity, and after the completion of his twelve canonical labors, he experienced his apotheosis on Olympus where, as an expression of gratitude, he was presented with Hebe, eternal youth. Hercules was considered the hero of virtue, who, in the famous story of choice between virtue and vice, conquered vice and achieved happiness in an exemplary manner. He was of exceptional significance amidst glorified rulers, particularly in the French court. The Gallic Hercules became synonymous with the French king and his virtues as ruler (fig. 21).[13]

By paying homage to her deceased husband Henri IV as Hercules in a funeral apotheosis, Marie de' Medici herself programmatically continued a symbolism for rulers in the Medici cycle that had been in use since Alexander the Great (fig. 22). The entrance of the king into heaven is not yet complete and already the reign of the queen widow is being festively acknowledged. The two events are simultaneously staged in one painting to effectively present the regent as guarantor of the continuity of dynastic rule.[14] The regent, dressed in black, sits elevated on the throne in front of a triumphal arch. The Amazon-like personification of France kneels before her and gives her the signifier of power, the imperial orb. The regent receives the rudder as ruler's symbol from the personification of divine foresight. Minerva stands armed directly behind the regent.

Given this context, it is likely that the regent was also alluding to her own particular situation with Vouet's scene of Hercules. Within the canon of heroic women, various women from antiquity, the Bible, or French history represented the takeover of male virtues and responsibilities. Lucretia defends her marriage with a courage usually associated with men. Zenobia and Joan of Arc reveal military strength. Semiramis, who is said to have achieved military success after posing as her son in men's clothing, undergoes a remarkable role reversal like Omphale. These heroines are introduced as role models in various polemics to show that women are by no means victims of their emotions, but rather, pursue higher goals. In Gabriel Gilbert's tragedy, published in 1647 and named after the heroine, Semiramis professes her passion to rule, "soif de régnier," a passion she values above the passion of love.[15] Hercules and Omphale could also be interpreted as the embodiment of two forms of passion in the context of a pro-woman Querelle des femmes. Omphale, spared Cupid's arrows, would then represent the passion of ruling, Hercules the passion of love. If one considers that Vouet's Omphale is not characterized as an off-putting dominatrix, neither in posture nor in gesture or facial expression, one could read this mythological subject as the regent's profession to this more noble passion of ruling.

In effect, several documents, originating in the French court, verify that the subject was being assessed anew at the time. In his 1633 text, *Devises et emblesmes d'amour moralisez*, Albert Flamen commented upon Hercules and Omphale with the words "*Semper aliquid—Jamais oisif*" [never idle] and interpreted the mythological pair as an example of inexhaustible industriousness.[16] The power of love, more precisely, the good

Fig. 22 Peter Paul Rubens, *The Apotheosis of Henri IV and the Proclamation of the Regency of Marie de Medici on May 4, 1610* (detail), 1622–25, oil on canvas, 394 × 727 cm (12 feet 11 in. × 23 feet 10¼ in.), Paris, Musée du Louvre

influence of women can bring this about. Georges de Scudéry agreed with this interpretation in his 1646 "Le cabinet ... premier partie."[17]

In the *Querelle des femmes*, within the context of the much-discussed topos of the power of love through female beauty, Omphale's seductive nudity in Vouet's painting gains a newly explosive force. The argument—that nature gave women a beautiful body and along with it the ability to seduce men to compensate for their physical weakness—was cited by many who supported the teachings of equality. Hercules and Omphale would then serve as an example that gender-specific strengths and weaknesses mutually presuppose and complement each other. Whenever the man proves himself to be weak, the woman shows her strength. Based on the premise that each sex has its strengths and weaknesses, Hercules and Omphale paradoxically do not stand for the superiority of one sex, but rather, for the equality of man and woman. This model of the two being complementary is essentially a variant of the aforementioned teaching of equality and equally maintains that human completeness is only possible in the unity of man and woman.

Minerva Pacifera—THE PACIFICATION OF SOCIETY THROUGH FEMALE RULE

Depending on the political situation, the regents employed both arguments. When proof of the equal value of the body politic was needed, they used the argument for gender equality. When the particular strengths of women were to be emphasized to foreground the advantage over male rule, then the argument of difference was cited.

In the long run, the iconography of Artemisia could not hold up as proof of equality, and thus the regents developed an iconography of Minerva that effectively presented proof of difference and was particularly emphasized in their commissioned work. A central motif in their visual propaganda was thereby the preservation of peace.

In an occasionally creatively disguised manner, the iconography suggests that successful rule must be based on the strength of the female sex and can only survive when peace, including peace between the sexes, reigns. When one sex is oppressed, society is robbed of its peace, and constructive collaboration between the sexes, essential to the preservation of the state's power, is prevented.

In his much-read work *Égalité des deux sexes* from 1673, Poulain de la Barre openly spells out these arguments and associates them with the concrete demands for a social utopia. He criticizes society's "fall from grace" as having created a hierarchy and division of labor that destroys peaceful coexistence. He demands that all humans be able to realize their potential without restrictions. He rejects militarily enforced pacification and sees the restoration of the equality of the sexes and the integration of women in all aspects of public life as a solution for the realization of a peaceful society.[18]

Christina of Sweden was also among those rulers who first and foremost propagated theirs as a rule of peace. In numerous writings and poems, she was celebrated as the peace-loving "Pallas of the Century." She herself wanted to go down in history as the one who brought about peace in Westphalia. To this end, she had a medallion stamped by Sebastian Dadler in 1649/50 showing her as *Minerva Pacifera* with an olive branch (fig. 23).[19]

Fig. 23 Sebastian Dadler, *Christina of Sweden as Minerva Pacifera*, reverse of medal, 1649/50, copper, 55 mm (2¼ in.) diam., Münster, Stadtmuseum Münster, MZ-WF-00100

In seventeenth-century emblems, Minerva, in the company of Mars, is expressly associated with the ruler and used to enhance the allegories for the ruler. In connection with Mars, Minerva, who was certainly known as a combative warrior, takes on the part of peacekeeper and becomes a patroness of the arts. In Gabriel Rollenhagen's book of emblems, Mars and Minerva are joined together as the personification of the ruler's virtues under the motto "*Arte et Marte*"; the accompanying verse states: "There are two who bring honor to the king/Art and the art of war/Fame comes from art as it does from the art of war."[20]

Since antiquity, the flourishing state was to be founded on *fortitudo et sapientia* (strength and wisdom). Based on this notion, the ideal of a ruling figure, in whom strength and erudition complemented each other meaningfully, was developed from the fourteenth century onward. Mars, and the victorious battles associated with him, no longer sufficed as a means to glorify power. Minerva, and the arts and sciences promoted by her, had to be added as well.[21]

In an emblem paying homage to the Habsburg emperor Charles V, Minerva's role as one who brings about peace and her important task as the emperor's advisor are commented upon in the following words: "... Brave Mars and wise Minerva lend active assistance to him [Emperor Charles V] / Weapons are of little use outside if intelligence does not rule inside ...."[22] Courage and wisdom are presented in opposition to one another and in relationship to the public ("outside" – battlefield) and private ("inside" – home) spheres.

In 1603 Guillaume Dupré created a medallion type for the French court, based on the agreement of virtues for the gods, that was minted subsequently many times (pl. 41). He shows the royal family in the guise of mythological figures under the motto "*Propago Imperi*" (The Offspring of the Empire): Marie de' Medici as Minerva in garments from antiquity, with shield and aegis; Henri IV as Mars with suit of armor, paludamentum, lance, and sword. Above Louis XIII (the heir to the throne), a putto with the father's helmet, and the dauphin, the couple extends each other a hand. Above them, Jupiter's eagle brings the crown.

In a commemorative medal from 1604 attributed to Philippe Danfrie the Younger, on the other hand, Henri IV as Mars and Marie de' Medici as Minerva are represented with the cornucopia of abundance. They extend their hands toward each other over a burning fire (pl. 93). The motto "*Maiestas Maior Ab Igne*" refers to the fact that unity between the sexes, brought together by the flame of love, strengthens the power of the state. In contrast to Rollenhagen's emblem, in which the virtues of Mars and Minerva are meant to represent a single ruling figure, the two French medallions each specify them in terms of gender and person. The warrior tasks and the related virtue of courage are ascribed to the king, the peaceful tasks to the queen. As purveyor of peace, she supports the arts, sciences, and crafts. Mars and Minerva's extending of hands is reminiscent of the *dextrarum iunctio*, an oath of loyalty that married couples gave to each other by joining their right hands. The gesture provides an interesting illustration of the aforementioned absorption of matters of private law into the realm of state law. It becomes apparent that a dual plane of references is suggested here. One applies to the concrete bond of the married couple and thus the body natural, the other to the pact between two body politics and to the union of two ruling virtues.

Fig. 24 Johann Blum, *William II of Orange and Mary of England*, obverse of medal, 1641, silver, 72 mm (2⅞ in.) diam., Amsterdam, Rijksmuseum

Fig. 25 Johann Blum, *William II of Orange and Mary of England as Minerva and Pax*, reverse of medal, 1641, silver, 72 mm (2⅞ in.) diam., Amsterdam, Rijksmuseum

Fig. 26 G. Grupello, *Grand Elector Johann Wilhelm von der Pfalz as Jupiter/Hercules and Queen Anne of England as Minerva*, from the Rapparini manuscript, Düsseldorf, Heinrich-Heine-Institut. Source: G.M. Rapparini, *Le portrait du vrai Mérite dans la Personne Serenissme de Monsigneur L'Electeur palatin*. Reprint Düsseldorf 1958, Pl. 11, medal no. 64, 1709, pen and ink, 80 mm (3⅛ in.) diam.

Danfrie's medallion represents a motto that was of central significance to numerous European monarchies: "Only in unity lies strength."[23] On the allegorical level the metaphor of the married couple served to demonstrate the inseparability of the state. To ensure this strength it is seen as sensible that the queen be drawn into the duties of the state and that her particular capabilities be utilized. The king's absence during war provides an important argument that the gender-specific allocation of tasks in the highest office be made as plausible as possible. In a clever manner, the necessity for the queen, as the country's representative, to assume care of the arts and sciences is justified. This medallion not only illustrates an important step in the integration of the female sex into the affairs of the state, it also takes a gender-specific visual message and fixes it as a symbol of strength in unity. In this unity, the man embodies war and courage, the woman peace and wisdom. Consequently, one finds this gender-specific allocation of state affairs and ruler's virtues in numerous European courts, with many female rulers going down in history as ambitious patrons of the arts and sciences.

The following two representations reveal the effect that Dupré's medallion had at several European courts. The first, a wedding medallion created in 1641 on the occasion of the marriage between William II of Orange and Mary of England, altered the French model to show the figures clad in contemporary attire on the obverse and in mythological garments on the reverse (figs. 24, 25). Interestingly, William appears here in the female form of Minerva, receiving an olive branch as a symbol of peace from Mary of England in the guise of Pax. Ceres accompanies Pax. Minerva seems far more warrior-like here with, one might say, masculine connotations. Surrounded by cannons and other instruments of war, she crushes Bellona, the goddess of war, who is lying on the ground beneath her. Within the historical context of the Thirty Years War and the struggle of the northern Netherlands against Spain, which had lasted almost eighty years, the allegorical meaning of the goddess as personification of the victory over Bellona was foregrounded to such an extent that even a ruler could present himself with dignity in this role. The gender of the goddess is completely irrelevant. The regent as Pax is presented as an indispensable ally and makes her contribution to the work of peace. Victorious Minerva and Pax, accompanied by Victory and Ceres, are combined here into one unity of strength.

The second example from 1709, in the manuscript of George Maria Rapparini, Language Secretary of Johann Wilhelm of the Pfalz, celebrates the Grand Elector as a Jupiter-like Hercules, who freed the Roman empire from the yoke of Louis XIV (fig. 26). The alliance with England is sealed in the sixty-fourth out of a total of 137 medallion-shaped drawings. Jan Wellem now sits hand-in-hand next to his English queen, Anne, who is depicted as the figure of Juno, dressed as Pallas. Juno is indicated by the peacock near Hercules and her helmet signifies Minerva. The inscription "*Una salvs ambobvs erit*" (To both the same salvation), though, attests to the strength in unity.

Over time, Hercules often took the place of Mars, thereby effecting a shift in the glorification of rulers from war heroes to heroes of virtue. By contrast, Minerva, as contributor to peace and personification of the "good reign" (as well as virginity, wisdom, and virtue), remained the favored role or companion for female regents up through the eighteenth century.[24]

Dupré's peace-bringing Minerva heralded a political self-understanding on the part of Marie de' Medici that is even more clearly and self-consciously propagated in the Medici cycle. After the king's murder, the queen commissioned Peter Paul Rubens to paint two painting cycles with two different subjects. Corresponding to the allocation of tasks depicted on the medallion, one theme represented the warlike victory of her husband in the guise of Hercules while the other testified to her own triumph as ruler of peace. Twenty-four mythological-allegorical scenes show the queen to be closely connected to Minerva on different levels. The main goal of this complex worldly apotheosis was to identify her as the legitimate successor to Henri IV. She celebrated the reconciliation with her son, after years of disagreement, and manifested her undiminished political presence. The painting cycle was inaugurated in a central position above the mantlepiece together with the large official portrait of herself as Minerva (pl. 22).[25] Minerva also befitted the young princess in the role of educator. In another scene, celebrating the end of the dispute regarding the succession of Juliers, the queen rides triumphantly on a white horse, Amazon-like and decorated with the attributes of Minerva. In all other events, Minerva serves her as advisor and protector.

GENDER REVERSAL IN THE ALLEGORICAL BODY?

In 1664 Anne of Austria had Simon Renard de Saint-André (1613–1677) paint an allegorical dual portrait of herself with her daughter-in-law, Maria Theresa, the oldest daughter of Philip IV of Spain and wife of Louis XIV, as Minerva and Pax (fig. 27).

Since allegories mostly occur in the female body, a complex mixture takes place in the allegorical portrait of a female ruler, so that person and idea are more closely interlocked than in the allegorical portraits of their male counterparts. In the portrait of a male ruler, on the other hand, the predominately female allegories are physically separate from him as his companions. The distribution of roles between the politically active men and the female embodiment of political goals and ideals is evident. As Kaulbach has shown, Pax is almost exclusively personified as female.[26] Only rarely does the male ruler slip into the female role. To avoid the risk of being ridiculed, he had to make clear that his person was standing in for a larger virtue and that he, as "ruler in the theatrical sense of the typical Baroque mentality,"[27] was merely appearing as a mediator of virtues. The virtues were not understood as a personal expression of the ruler, but rather as the personification of the institutional dynastic body. Thus the persons bearing these ruler's virtues were exchangeable, whereas the virtues themselves as inherited aptitudes were to remain as the dynasty's constant defining trait. This notion of a genealogy of virtues was to justify the continuity of the dynasty.

Under no circumstance does the ruler undergo gender reversal when he slips into a female role. Rather, the female goddess or allegorized virtue loses her sexuality and is neutralized as dynastic sign or concept. Cesare Ripa commented on this in his *Iconologia*: Strength "should be a Lady, not to declare thereby that a strong man should come close to feminine ways, but to make the figure suit the way we speak; or on the other hand, as every virtue is an appearance of the true, the beautiful and the desirable, in which the

Fig. 27 Simon Renard de Saint-André, *Portrait of Anne of Austria as Minerva and Queen Maria Theresa as Pax*, c. 1660, oil on canvas, 130 × 111 cm (51⅛ × 43¾ in.), Versailles, Musée nationale des Châteaux de Versailles et de Trianon

intellect take its delight, and as we commonly attribute beauty to the ladies, we can conveniently represent one by the other; or rather because, just as those women who deprive themselves of the pleasures to which nature has made them incline acquire and preserve the glory of an exceptional honour, so the strong man, risking his body, putting his life in danger, his soul aflame with virtue, gives birth to reputation and fame of the highest esteem."[28]

Constantine II was already an admirer of Minerva in antiquity and assumed her guise. The gold medal from Nicomedia of 353–361 shows him with a gorgoneion, lance, and a small statue of Victoria in his hand. In the Calendar of Ficocalus of 354, which we know in a reproduction of a Carolingian copy from 1620–29 in the Vatican collection in Rome, Gallus Caesar, the new consul of the year 354, represents himself as a standing Minerva with a lance and also with a small statue of Victoria. This served as a model for Marie de' Medici's opening portrait as Minerva in the Medici cycle.[29] In an anonymous copy after a miniature by Niccolò dell'Abate (1509–1571) in the Bibliothèque nationale, François I was even depicted as a bearded Minerva with the attributes of the gods Mercury, Diana, Amor and Mars (pl. 45).

There is, however, no indication that the inverse occurred, that is, of female regents being represented as gods such as Mars or Hercules or as male allegories. Two explanations for this are possible: first, it could mean that male god figures could not be as easily neutralized into a sign as female figures. Obviously, the gender of Hercules and Mars continued to be of significance to their divine form. It could also indicate that the gender of the female regent whether in a mythological or allegorical body, was still considered of prime importance.

The first sign of allegorization in male guise, though, can be detected in the visual propaganda of two queens. Christina of Sweden and Elizabeth I were both partially linked to Hercules' allegorical context. The deceased Swedish king Gustav II Adolf, who, in an apotheosis, is lifted up to heaven as Hercules by Jupiter's eagle, gives his daughter Christina of Sweden Hercules' club, instead of a scepter, as a symbol of strength (pl. 48). A gender reversal, however, does not take place here: unlike her father, Christina is not represented as a Swedish Hercules. She merely takes on the attributes of male strength to prove that the continuity of Sweden's superior military might is ensured through her.

In 1596 Crispin van de Passe the Elder portrayed Elizabeth I of England, standing between two columns in a full-length engraving (pl. 20). Here, the English queen is placed within the tradition of Charles V, who, on several occasions, had himself represented as Hercules with the two columns as a symbol of strength.[30] It is noteworthy that the male virtue of strength is validated for a woman in the king's office. This was only possible because it concerned the body politic, not the actual person, representing interests that transcend gender, namely the kingdom's imperial power politics.

By comparison, a noteworthy play with androgyny and gender reversal is evident in a mythologically-charged portrait of the English queen, attributed to Hans Eworth (fig. 28).[31] In this variation on the judgement of Paris, the queen's gender reversal is not visible, but rather, is apparent by association. The informed viewer recognizes in her the figure of Paris, even though she appears as queen in the form of a female body in a costly dress. This artfully disguised role-playing suggests an association both with the

Fig. 28 Attributed to Hans Eworth, *Elizabeth I and the Three Goddesses*, 1569, oil on panel, 70.8 × 84.5 cm (27⅞ × 33¼ in.), East Molesey, Hampton Court Palace

male hero of antiquity and with the political body of state, that is, with the queen bearing crown and imperial orb, as well as the queen's body natural as chosen female beauty. The figure of the queen oscillates between the gendered, political and allegorical body and between the portrait of a ruling individual, state portrait and allegorized ruler. By chasing the three goddesses out of the temple with the imperial orb as royal sign of power, she places herself as secular person above the divinities, the most important goddesses of antiquity. In the panegyrian portrait, the English queen, not the three goddesses, is assigned the prize of the golden apple, thereby taking first place in the beauty contest. Thus, she is both judged object and judging subject in one person. In the place of Paris, but not in his role, and as an expression of her absolute sovereignty, she decides who is the most beautiful and powerful woman in the kingdom. As in the case of mythological figures such as the virginal Astraea or the self-immolating and self-procreating Phoenix (pl. 66),[32] Elizabeth is given a high degree of autonomy here with regard to her sex's choice between virginal asexuality and androgyny.

Since each regent could easily be mistaken for the female allegory in these images, she was well-advised to constructively use the blending of actual person and embodiment of an idea for the purpose of her own visual propaganda. The dual portrait of Anne of Austria and Maria Theresa is more than a personal acknowledgment of the friendly relationship between mother-in-law and daughter-in-law. The representative portrait reflects the regent's ruling ideology and conveys an important political message. With the conclusion of the Thirty Years War in 1648, France under Anne of Austria had become a leading power next to Sweden. The war between France and Spain continued to be waged until 1659, however, and was only ended to the advantage of France with the Pyrenean Peace Accord, whereby France gained territory and power. This peace was finally secured in 1660 through the marriage of Louis XIV to the daughter of the Spanish king. One year later Anne of Austria passed on to her son the rule of a country at peace. The dual portrait was created two years before her death, demonstratively avowing the regent's politics of peace and representing, in particular, the peace with Spain for which she had pushed. As the pledge of peace, Maria Theresa personifies prosperity-bringing Pax. She supports Anne of Austria, "*la sage et grande Minerve*" (the wise and great Minerva) and the real *Minerva Pacifera*, in her politics of peace. Here, Dupré's symbol of strength through unity between the sexes, embodied in the ruling pair of Mars and Minerva, becomes a symbol of two members of the same sex signifying a positive female reign. By replacing Mars with Pax and having the former regent's prospective successor sit in the place of the male ruler, the painting suggests that one could do without male rule and that, instead and contrary to Salic law, the line of succession could pass between female regents. The male ruler's virtue of courage is superseded by the female ruler's virtue of pacifism. In their alliance and in the gesture of *dextrarum iunctio*, the former and the prospective rulers confirm the unity and strength of ruling by female genealogy. As patroness of peace, a maternal Minerva looks after the virginal figure of peace because, as Peter Paul Rubens had already shown in an allegory, it is Minerva's duty to protect Pax against Mars.[33] In this context, one can read the dual portrait as a disguised genealogy of virtues of female rule. At issue here is no longer the idea that Minerva and Mars complement one another, but rather, that women might have particular strength when it comes to matters of peace. In the period of pacifism following the Westphalian armistice, the warlike "male" strength of Mars was no longer sought after but was replaced by the female Pax. The claim that women are superior peacemakers over men is hidden under the guise of the allegorized dual virtues.

The last and final example also shows that although one could never fully dissociate the regent from her gender, gender could be used advantageously in the visual propaganda. In an engraving by Thomas de Leu, Marie de' Medici is portrayed as the crown of justice (pl. 47). By reuniting the separate functions of the king and the law in her person, she not only surpasses the boundaries of her gender, but also of her office. As the personification of justice, she sits on her throne, ruling *en majesté*, as the inscription below the image explains, over the body and limbs, kings, armies, laws, peace, and militia. Dressed in the royal ermine, decorated with lilies, she demonstrates the strength of the unity between law and the office of the king. She also represents the French kingship as guarantor of the rule of law. Not surprisingly, the representation recalls the *lit de justice* (The Seat of Justice), the celebratory summoning of parliament, during which the king, sitting under a canopy, practiced his sovereign and absolute power. As mediator between heaven and earth, it is useful for Marie de' Medici that she and the female personification of justice share the same sex, allowing her to become the living embodiment of the highest possible enthronement.[34]

Le Moyne's imperative "The king is genderless" and Poulain de la Barre's crucial statement in his polemic on women's rights that "reason is genderless" followed the phrase "talent is genderless," coined by the painter A. Renon, Secretary of the Royal Academy, in defense of female artists. Madame de Staël's subsequent famous remark that talent is genderless—"*Le talent n'a point sexe*"[35]—remained an influential argument in the seemingly never-ending debate between the sexes. For female regents back then and for women today, gender remains both a burden and an opportunity.

This essay was translated from the German by Karein Goertz.

NOTES

1   Kantorowicz 1994; Bredekamp 1998; and Bredekamp 1999.

2   Kantorowicz 1994, pp. 212ff.

3   The exhibition "Die Galerie der starken Frauen, La Gallerie des femmes fortes: Die Heldin in der französischen und italienischen Kunst des 17. Jahrhunderts," curated by Bettina Baumgärtel and Silvia Neysters (Baumgärtel and Neysters 1995), sought to classify the configurations and representational forms of female power in seventeenth-century art.

4   Gaehtgens 1995. For a discussion of some of the theses, see Baumgärtel 1997.

5   See Zimmermann's groundbreaking essay "Vom Streit der Geschlechter: Die französische und italienische Querelle des femmes des 15. bis 17. Jahrhunderts." (Zimmermann 1995); Bock and Zimmermann 1997.

6   Gössmann 1984.

7   De Gournay 1989, p. 74, cited in Zimmermann 1995, p. 33.

8   Maclean 1977, p. 217, fig. 8.

9   There are many references to the reductive arguments of moral theologians; see Baader 1995 and Die Galerie der starken Frauen 1995, pp. 140–81, cat. no. 55.

10 Die Galerie der starken Frauen 1995, pp. 153–57.

11 The painting, considered missing, was engraved by Michel Dorigny in 1643. Compare Die Galerie der starken Frauen 1995, pp. 155f.

12 Attention has already been drawn to this in Kantorowicz 1994, pp. 503ff, fig. 32a.

13 Vivanti 1968.

14 See Millen and Wolf 1989, pl. 38.

15 Gilbert 1647. See Maclean 1977, p. 181.

16 Maclean 1977, pp. 217f, fig 10.

17 Ibid.

18 Gössmann 1984, p. 16. For a critical analysis, see Steinbrügge 1987.

19 On the subject of Minerva, see Dowley 1955; Wittkower, "Der Wandel des Minerva-Bildes in der Renaissance," in Wittkower 1984, pp. 246–70, 399–402; Pfeiff 1987; Warner 1985.

20 Rollenhagen 1611. See also Henkel and Schöne 1967, p. 1739.

21 Brink 2000.

22 Anneau 1552, p. 116; see also Pfeiff 1987.

23 This motto has a long tradition in the self-conception of the monarchies and also determined the two bodies doctrine; see Kantorowicz 1994, pp. 212ff. Interestingly, Hercules embodied this motto in The Netherlands' struggle for independence, as Holmann (1991–92) has shown.

24 See Pfeiff 1987.

25 Pfeiff (1987, pp. 6, 91) has pointed to the questionable interpretation of Bellona; see also Wittkower 1984 and Kaulbach 1994, p. 42, wherein Bellona is interpreted as representing Minerva's warlike side that, in contrast to Mars, stands for wise, well-considered actions in war.

26 Kaulbach 1994, pp. 27–49.

27 Matsche 1981, p. 63.

28 Ripa 1602, pp. 90–93, cited in Warner 1985, p. 65.

29 Pfeiff 1987, pp. 6, 41–42, figs. 35–36.

30 For a more detailed analysis, see Yates 1947, pp. 52, 55–75, 81, n. 1, fig. 17g.

31 Yates (1947, pp. 60f, fig. 19a) refers to a poem by Barnfield, Fairy Queen, in which not Paris, but Elizabeth I as Jove receives the golden ball.

32 Ibid.

33 Pax was typically represented as innocence dressed in white and as a beautiful virgin. In honor of the conclusion of a peace mission in 1629–1630, Peter Paul Rubens gave the English king an allegory, Minerva protects Pax from Mars ("Peace and War") (Kaulbach 1994, pp. 46–47).

34 For more on the subject of lit de justice and "living justice," see Kantorowicz 1994, pp. 139f. and 414f.

35 Antoine Renon, Journal de Paris, Nr. 190, 9 June 1785, S. 789.

41

GUILLAUME DUPRÉ
French, c. 1576–1643
Louis XIII as Dauphin between Henri IV as Mars and Marie de' Medici as Minerva, reverse of medal

1603
Gilt bronze
68 mm (2¾ in.) diam., with loop
National Gallery of Art, Washington,
Samuel H. Kress Collection 1957

The reverse side of this medal made by court medalist Guillaume Dupré shows Henri IV and his wife Marie de' Medici clasping hands. He is shown in the guise of Mars, god of war, and she is represented as Minerva, goddess of wisdom and the arts. Between them stands their young son, the Dauphin Louis XIII. The inscription PROPAGO IMPERI, "the offspring of the empire," refers to the dynastic ambitions of the royal couple.

42

GEORG PENCZ

German, c. 1500–1550

Artemisia Preparing to Drink Her Husband's Ashes

c. 1539
Engraving
191 × 135 mm (7½ × 5⅜ in.)
San Francisco, Fine Arts Museums of San Francisco, Achenbach Foundation for Graphic Arts

Artemisia was the virtuous widow of Mausolus, who succeeded her husband as ruler of Caria in Asia Minor after his death, and had a great monument built in his memory (the "mausoleum"). In Pencz's engraving, Artemisia sits in a private chamber, preparing to drink her potion of ashes, while her husband's funeral pyre burns outside. Her solemn expression, the articles of Mausolus's armor surrounding her, and the quiet, shadowed interior suggest a state of mourning. The vessel that sits on the window sill alludes to the notion that her body will become a vessel, a living tomb, as Valerius Maximus wrote, for her husband's remains.

43

GERRIT VAN HONTHORST

Dutch, 1592–1656

Artemisia

1632–35
Oil on canvas
170 × 147.5 cm (67 × 58 in.)
Princeton, The Art Museum, Princeton University, Museum purchase, gift of George L. Craig, Class of 1921, and Mrs. Craig

Honthorst's painting depicts a moment from the story of Artemisia recounted by Valerius Maximus, in which she drank her husband's ashes, mixed in a liquid. Thus, Artemisia, according to Valerius, made herself a living, breathing tomb. This widow of ancient history was considered a symbol of a widow's devotion to her husband, and was often held up as a role model or precedent by later widowed queens.

Te clauam mutare colo cum cerneret, Heros,
Hæc matri referam ludicra: dixit Amor.

S. Vouet pinxit   cum priuileg. Regis   M. Dorigny Sc. 1643

Francoys en guerre est vn Mars furieux
En paix Minerue & diane a la chasse
A bien parler Mercure copieux
A bien aymer vray Amour. plein de grace
O france heureuse honore donc la face
De ton grand Roy qui surpasse Nature
Car l'honorant tu sers en mesme place
Minerue. Mars. Diane. Amour. Mercure

45
After NICCOLÒ
DELL'ABATE
Italian, 1509/12–1571
Portrait of François I

16th century
Engraving
227 × 190 mm (10⅞ × 7½ in.)
Paris, Bibliothèque nationale de
France

This engraving after a miniature
depicting François I combines
attributes of Minerva, Mars,
Diana, and Cupid in a complex
and enigmatic image. The king
wears the helmet and
Gorgoneion breastplate of
Minerva; he holds in his right
hand the sword of Mars, whose
armor covers his arm; the
caduceus and winged sandals
belong to Mercury; he bears the
horn of Diana, and the bow and
quiver of either Cupid or Diana.
While the image's androgyny is
unmistakable, and has been
much remarked on, its precise
significance is debated.

44
MICHEL DORIGNY
French, 1617–1665
After SIMON VOUET
French, 1590–1649
Hercules and Omphale

1643
Engraving with etching
217 × 159 mm (8½ × 6⅜ in.)
Paris, Bibliothèque nationale de France

Dorigny has portrayed Hercules
and Omphale in a moment of
gender reversal. Hercules has
taken on feminine attributes—he
spins, traditionally considered an
activity emblematic of women's
work—and Omphale drapes him
in her clothing. With Hercules's
club and lion skin at her feet,
Omphale holds a whip and lash,
apparently a further reference to
her domination of the hero.

46
LÉONARD GAULTIER
French, 1561–1641
After NICOLAS
BOLLERY
French, active 1585, died 1630
The Coronation of Marie de' Medici

1610
Engraving
262 × 336 mm (10¼ × 13¼ in.)
Paris, Bibliothèque nationale de France

Marie de' Medici was crowned Queen of France at Saint-Denis on May 13, 1610, just one day before her husband, Henri IV, was assassinated. The print records myriad details of the ceremony, in which Marie is shown in full regalia. Her courtly retinue included the Dauphin, Louis XIII, as well as other members of the extended royal family and courtiers.

LA COURONNE

DE JUSTICE.

fournier. pinx.
Thomas de Leu fecit.

Celle je suis qui fais regner les Roys   Et maintenir la Paix et la Milice
Qui scay regir les Armes et les Loix   En corrigeant des hommes la malice.

47
THOMAS DE LEU
French, *c.* 1555–1612
After ISAÏE FOURNIER
French, 17th century
*Portrait of Marie de'
Medici as Justice*
1609
engraving
198 × 144 mm (7¾ × 5⅝ in.) plate
Cambridge, Fogg Art Museum,
Harvard University Art Museums,
Jakob Rosenberg Fund

Marie de' Medici appears in de
Leu's print as an allegory of
Justice, holding the scales and
the sword of justice, and clad
conspicuously in robes decorated
with the fleur-de-lis. It is
interesting that such an image
of Marie embodying this virtue
of a leader should appear in
1609, as she had not yet
assumed the throne as regent
(her husband Henri IV was not
assassinated until 1610). In Peter
Paul Rubens's painting *The
Felicity of the Regency*, a canvas in
his painting cycle of the life of
Marie (1622–25), she also holds
the scales of Justice.

48

JEREMIAS FALCK
Polish, c. 1610
After SÉBASTIEN
BOURDON
French, 1616–1671
178 × 280 mm
(7 × 11 in.)

Christina receives the
Herculean Arms from
Gustav II Adolf, as Fame
Records Swedish Victory
in Germany, title page
to Bogislav Philipp von
Chemnitz, Koeniglichen
Schwedischen in
Teutschland gefuehrten
Krieges…, vol. 2,
Stockholm,
J. Janssonius, 1653

Engraving
New Haven, The Beinecke Rare Book
and Manuscript Library, Yale
University

Christina was the famously
politically astute and highly
cultured queen of Sweden, who
was crowned when she was only
eighteen. In this frontispiece to
Chemnitz's history of Sweden's
wars in Germany, Christina is
shown receiving the Herculean
arms – a club and lion skin –
from her father, the late King
Gustav II Adolf, who appears as
Zeus. Associating Christina with
these conventional symbols of
masculine prowess acknowledges
the unusual nature of her
position and powers. At the same
time, the image implies that her
power to rule is dependent on
Gustav, even though Christina
had ruled successfully on her
own for nine years.

Women Who Ruled: Queens, Goddesses, Amazons 1500–1650 A Thematic Overview

ANNETTE DIXON

During the period 1500–1650, the phenomenon of large numbers of women ruling challenged gender boundaries. Images played an important part in women's assertion of power beyond traditional, sanctioned roles. Women's rule brought to the fore long-standing disputes about the appropriateness of women wielding control over their own destinies, along with newer concerns about the suitability of women exercising authority over others—whether in the state or the household. Patrons and artists who sought to advocate for female activity understood that images were potent vehicles for reflecting and shaping opinions on the empowerment of women. So, too, did those made anxious by the idea of women in power turn to the visual arts to lament the transgressions of the social order and to reinforce male prerogatives. The thematic organization of this exhibition allows us to examine a rich assortment of nearly 100 works according to women's social roles as they reflect both the traditional place of women in their societies and as they reflect the expansion of notions of what was woman's proper place.

The familiar categories of wife, mother, and virgin represent traditional roles for women in patriarchal societies. Within these typically subjugated roles, women found ways to project power and to be exemplars of socially sanctioned ideals of womanhood. By contrast, sexually assertive women, who rejected traditional constraints imposed on women, were viewed as dangerous to society. The commingling of elements of seduction and heroism, particularly in frequently represented Biblical heroines such as Judith, suggests a deep-seated ambivalence to strong women.

Women rulers who moved outside traditional arenas of female power sought to assert their authority beyond socially prescribed roles by having themselves represented as goddesses or showing themselves in the traditionally masculine role of warrior. Women's influence and the spectrum of reactions it fostered brought opportunities to rethink conventions of representation—in portraiture, narrative, and allegory. In the pages that follow we examine the revision of conventions through an analysis of a selection of artwork from this period. The great number of media represented—paintings, drawings, prints, book illustration, sculpture, and the decorative arts—reveals the degree to which concerns with the empowerment and marginalization of women penetrated the visual culture of the time.

Opposite: Aegidius Sadeler after Bartholomäus Spranger,
The Triumph of Wisdom over Ignorance, c. 1600 (pl. 87, detail)

I. WIVES AND MOTHERS

The depiction of female consorts in various roles—spouse, married sexual partner, child-bearer, or ensurer of dynasty—reflects the chief functions of these rulers' wives: to produce male progeny in order to carry the dynastic line forward (pls. 49, 50) and to represent her husband in his absence. These depictions may stress the female ruler's deference to her husband, her maternity, or her widowhood and continuing link to him after his death. They encompass state portraits as well as the more domestic and intimate side of self-representation.

A key example of the state portrait, which expressed the female ruler's importance to the concept of dynasty, is Agnolo Bronzino's painting of Eleanora of Toledo, seen here in an artist's copy from the Detroit Institute of Arts of the original of 1545 now in the Uffizi Gallery (pl. 51).[1] Daughter of the Spanish viceroy to Naples, she married Duke Cosimo I de' Medici in 1539, and in 1541 he declared her regent. Bronzino's painting commemorates both her authority as regent and her role in the dynasty. This portrait, created as pendant to Bronzino's portrait of her husband in armor, is the first state portrait painting to show a wife along with her son, establishing an important trend in the official portraiture of female rulers (see, for example, the painting by Justus Sustermans of a later Medici mother and child, Maria Maddalena of Austria and her young son, pl. 52). The inclusion of a male child (whether it is the eldest and heir, Francesco, born in 1541, or Giovanni, born in 1543), stresses her role as progenitor and ensurer of the Medici dynasty. Eleanora of Toledo is posed regally, eyeing the viewer with an assured stare. The imposing quality is enhanced by her magnificent, close-fitting costume with its dazzling pattern. It has been argued that the material used for the dress is a brocaded satin made in Florence rather than in Spain (though it is based on a Spanish design), making this painting an assertion of state identity as embodied in the female ruler.[2]

In contrast, a miniature by Giulio Clovio made less than a decade after the formal portrait (seen in the exhibition in a later copy by Daniel Fröschl), gives a different view of Eleanora.[3] As a private rather than official record of the queen, this work is itself intimate in scale and tone, a quality achieved through the gentle way in which she looks at the viewer, the modest gesture of her hand resting below her bustline, and her less elaborate costume. A more severe image of Eleanora is seen in a bust of 1544 by Baccio Bandinelli modeled after ancient Roman imperial matrons.[4]

While portraits of female consorts made while husbands were alive stressed the wife's fecundity and concern for the royal family, it was during a widow's regency that a queen had to assert herself in assuring the successful accession to power of her young son, and in playing a more active role in the court and the state. While the tutelage of the child was traditionally up to her, the queen often had to fight to preserve her right to be regent. Imagery could play an important role in bolstering her power. Imagery of mature women rulers such as Catherine de' Medici, her distant relative Marie de' Medici, and the latter's daughter-in-law Anne of Austria—all of whom ruled as queen regents after the deaths of their husbands—tends to project a sense of a widow's decorum and her firm support of the heir's right to rule—and, by extension, her own claim to regency. They devised a variety of stratagems, sometimes featuring their maternality

Opposite: Justus Sustermans, *Maria Maddalena of Austria (Wife of Duke Cosimo II de' Medici) with her Son, the Future Ferdinand II, c.* 1623 (pl. 52, detail)

Fig. 29 Antoine Caron, *The Distribution of the Book and the Sword*, late 16th century, oil on panel, 51 × 73 cm (20⅛ × 28¾ in.), Beauvais, Musée départemental de l'Oise

or widowhood, sometimes identifying with women from the Bible or history whom they adopted as role models. Through their patronage, exchanges of gifts, and displays of largesse—in the commissioning of portraits in the form of paintings or medals, and in the planning of and participation in ceremonial aspects of queenship such as royal entries and festivities—they made statements that related to the legitimacy of their rule and the power of their queenship.

Following the deaths of their husbands, regents had themselves portrayed in widows' garb (pls. 53–56, 58), both in memory of the deceased and as a way to stress the marital link that gave them power. Rather than relinquish widow's garments after the required period of mourning, Catherine de' Medici wore hers for the rest of her life, thereby distinguishing herself from all the other ladies in her court. At a time when the color of widows' dress was variable, Catherine chose black, the color worn by Catholic male monarchs of the period.[5]

As a regent Catherine took an active role raising her son, making sure he was educated in the princely arts and ready to govern. Yet rather than show herself in this central role and risk provoking the jealousy of conniving courtiers, on the advice of her court adviser, Nicholas Houel, Catherine adopted the persona of Artemisia in her images.[6] This queenly predecessor, widow of Mausolus, the ruler of ancient Caria in Asia Minor, expressed loyalty to her dead husband through her actions (pls. 42, 43). A painting, one of several made by Catherine's court artist, Antoine Caron, for a cycle of tapestries on the story of Artemisia, shows the heroine towering over everyone else, placed in the center of the action, yet behind her son, the young king, symbolically promoting his power and ensuring her own (fig. 29).[7] Catherine's use of Artemisia inspired later rulers to adopt the same carefully crafted public alter-ego, including Marie de' Medici.

Comparing images made before and after the death of Henri IV brings out changes in the way Marie de' Medici's role as wife was depicted, reflecting her change in status and power. The family of Henri IV and Marie de' Medici is portrayed in a print of 1602 by Léonard Gaultier. This engraving of the royal family from a few years after their marriage celebrates the birth of the heir to the throne and stresses the subservient role of the queen (pl. 59).[8] The focus is on the relationship between the king and the young future king, the Dauphin Louis XIII. He is shown sitting on the lap of his nurse, who is seated just before the queen. The king, surrounded by nobles and flanked on his right by his illegitimate son César, is seated to the right of the queen. The king, gazing at his heir, extends his hand to him, cutting across the figure of the queen. Marie, separated from the largely male grouping on the right, looks directly out toward the viewer. She is clearly a subordinate figure and her role as childbearer is made evident by the grouping of figures and their interrelationships.

Prints of Marie following the assassination of Henri in 1610 show her with greater political power. An engraving by the same artist, created in 1613, lauds the queen regent's success in international diplomacy (pl. 60).[9] The majesty of the queen is expressed by her lavish dress and the sumptuous surroundings. The year before she had negotiated the betrothal of the young Dauphin and his future wife, Anne of Austria, the daughter of King Philip III of Spain. Here gathered around Marie are her female children. The female side on the left is balanced against a predominantly male side on the right with the young Dauphin and Anne of Austria, and the young king's attendants.

By contrast, a tender mood is conveyed by a portrait medallion showing Anne of Austria with her young son Louis XIV (pl. 57).[10] Court medalist Jean Warin produced this portrait in 1643 to commemorate the coming to the throne of the five-year-old Louis. It shows his mother, Anne of Austria, embracing her son. Her husband, Louis XIII, had tried to prevent her from becoming regent at his death by providing in his will for a council of regency. This council was overturned, however, and Anne was declared sole regent. Heretofore relegated to the sidelines, she suddenly found herself at the center of the court's attentions; she devoted herself, with the help of her advisor Cardinal Mazarin, to safeguarding her son's power.

49

THOMAS DE LEU

French, c. 1555–1612

After FRANÇOIS

QUESNEL

French, 1542/5–1619

Portrait of Henri IV

c. 1600

Engraving

205 × 130 mm (8⅛ × 5⅛ in.)

Paris, Bibliothèque nationale de

France

· MARIE DE MEDICIS ROYNE DE FRANCE ET DE NAVARRE ·

Les françois te peindront à la posterité
De Manteau, de couronne, et de Septre enrichie.
Parce qu'ilz ont receu de ta begninité
Des Rois, pour commander à cette monarchie.

Thomas de
Leu.excu.

Francoys Ques
nel, pyncct.

50

THOMAS DE LEU
French, c. 1555–1612
After FRANÇOIS
QUESNEL
French, 1542/5–1619
Portrait of Marie de'
Medici

c. 1600
Engraving
206 × 139 mm (8⅛ × 5½ in.)
Paris, Bibliothèque nationale de
France

A number of pendant portraits
of Marie de' Medici and her
husband, Henri IV, were
produced by de Leu in the years
following their marriage in
1600. In this pair, the verses
beneath Henri's image stress his
role as a just and rightful king,
while those accompanying
Marie's portrait refer to her
childbearing role as royal
consort.

51

AGNOLO BRONZINO
Italian, 1503–1572

Eleanora of Toledo and Her Son

c. 1545
Oil on panel
121.8 × 100 cm (47⅞ × 39⅜ in.)
Detroit, The Detroit Institute of Arts,
Gift of Mrs. Ralph Harman Booth in
memory of her husband, Ralph
Harman Booth

Eleanora of Toledo, Duchess of
Florence, was the wife of the
powerful Duke Cosimo I de'
Medici. Bronzino's state portrait
shows her posed regally, eyeing
the viewer with a steady, even
icy, stare. Her magnificent dress
of expensive brocaded satin
enhances the imposing, iconic
quality of her image, while the
presence of her young son
stresses her role as progenitor
and ensurer of the continuation
of the Medici dynasty.

52

JUSTUS SUSTERMANS
Flemish, 1597–1681

Maria Maddalena of Austria (Wife of Duke Cosimo II de' Medici) with her Son, the Future Ferdinand II

c. 1623
Oil on canvas
150 × 121.5 cm (58⅜ × 47¾ in.)
Flint, Collection of the Flint Institute of Arts, Gift of Mr. and Mrs. William L. Richards, 1965

After the death of her husband, Cosimo II de' Medici, Maria Maddalena of Austria ruled as co-regent, along with her mother, Christine of Lorraine, until her son Ferdinand came of age. Although this portrait was commissioned while Cosimo was alive, it was not finished until after his death. By picturing Maria Maddalena in her wedding dress with her heir, Sustermans emphasized her role in the continuation of the Medici dynasty. The painting is one of several copies Sustermans made after his original canvas, now in the Uffizi Gallery, to be disseminated in courtly circles.

53

THOMAS DE LEU

French, *c.* 1555–*c.* 1612

Portrait of Catherine de' Medici

Late 16th century

Engraving

147 × 98 mm (5⅞ × 3⅞ in.) sheet, trimmed to platemark

Lent by the Museum of Fine Arts, Boston, Gift of Gordon Abbott and George P. Gardner

As a queen mother, Catherine exercised strong influence over royal policies during the reigns of her sons François II, Charles IX, and Henri III. She played an important and controversial role in the politics of the Wars of Religion and was a great patron of the arts. Here she is depicted wearing widow's garments in black, a color she wore long after mourning to associate herself with Catholic male monarchs.

CATHERINE DE MEDICIS REYNE MERE DV ROY

Tous les Siecles paßez des Royautéz humeines,
Nont rien veu de pareil au vray de ce Tableau:
Ceft la Mere des Roys, et la Reyne des Reynes,
Qui par feś grands effetz, depite fon Tombeau.
Tho. de l. Fe. et ex

54

GUILLAUME MARTIN
French, 1558–c. 1590
Portrait of Catherine de'
Medici, reverse of
medal

1565
Struck silver
37 mm (1½ in.) diam.
Paris, Bibliothèque nationale de
France

Catherine de' Medici appears on
the reverse of the medal, while
her son Charles IX is depicted
on the obverse. Multiple copies
of the medal are believed to have
been produced as gifts for
Spanish notables at Catherine's
great festival at Bayonne during
the royal tour of France between
1564 and 1566. The
representation of Catherine in
profile view all'antica creates a
sense of authority, calling to
mind Roman imperial imagery.

55

GUILLAUME DUPRÉ
French, c. 1576–1643
Christine of Lorraine, Grand Duchess of Tuscany, uniface medal

1609–36
Cast bronze
93 mm (3⅝ in.) diam.
Los Angeles, Los Angeles County
Museum of Art

Christine of Lorraine, daughter of Charles III of Lorraine, was raised at the French court by her grandmother, Catherine de' Medici. She married Ferdinand I de' Medici, grand duke of Tuscany, who ruled between 1587 and 1609). She wears relatively subdued mourning clothes, the deep folds of her veil calling attention to her status as widow.

56

LÉONARD GAULTIER

French, 1561–1641

Portrait of Marie de' Medici

1610

Engraving

136 × 80 mm (5⅜ × 3⅛ in.)

Paris, Bibliothèque nationale de France

Gaultier's engraving was produced in 1610, the year in which Marie de' Medici became regent to her son, Louis XIII, after the assassination of her husband, Henri IV. By representing Marie in the costume of a widow, the portrait by Gaultier stressed the continuity between Henri's reign and the regency, thus affirming the queen's authority and her son's succession.

57

Attributed to

JEAN WARIN III

French, c. 1604–1672

Anne of Austria and Her Son, The Future King Louis XIV of France, uniface medallion

1643

Cast, chased, and patinated bronze
94 mm (3¾ in.) diam.
110 mm (4⅜ in.) height
including hanging finial
The Art Institute of Chicago,
Restricted Gift of Dr. Maxwell Reed
Mowry and Mr. and Mrs. George O.
Klotter, and the Russell Tyson Fund

Showing Anne of Austria
tenderly embracing her son,
this medal commemorates the
coming to the throne of the
five-year-old king. Her husband,
Louis XIII, had tried to prevent
her from becoming regent at his
death by providing in his will
for a council of regency. Anne
got the council overturned and
had herself proclaimed sole
regent.

58

JEAN MORIN

French, 1605/10–1650

After PHILIPPE DE
CHAMPAIGNE

French, 1602–1674

**Portrait of Anne of
Austria**

1645–50
Etching and engraving
300 × 248 mm (11⅞ × 9¾ in.)
plate, 471 × 347 mm
(18½ × 14⅞ in.) sheet
National Gallery of Canada, Ottawa,
Purchased 1950

Based on a painted portrait, this
print speaks to the importance of
disseminating the queen's image.
Wearing elegant mourning
clothes and adorned with
discreet, yet resplendent jewels,
Anne of Austria is identified here
as queen regent, and her
expression and bearing convey
self-possession.

O que ce prince crost, les enfans des Monarques
Qui sont les filz de Dieu ne tardent a venir,
Du Roy son Pere il a et les traicaz et les marques
Puisse il vn jour son heur et ses vertus tenir.

Dieu vueille que de tout a son Pere il resemble,
Affin qu'il soit l'hercule et le mars des francois,
Qu'a ses septres acquis des conquis il assemble,
Les gagnant par son bras les gardant par ses lois

Le Ciel qui m'a donné deux septres par ma dextre,
Se souuenant de moy le fauorisera,
Ie croy qu'on le verra aultant qu'Alexandre estre,
Et que tout l'vniuers ne le contentera.

Ie croisteray ce pendant pour luy faire seruice,
Fidelle consacrant ma vie a son besoing,
Indigne ie seroys que d'vn Roy ie naquisse,
Si de son filz dauphin aux combatz sestois loing.

59
LÉONARD GAULTIER
French, 1561–1641
The Family of Henri IV

1602
Engraving
252 × 312 mm (9⅞ × 12¼ in.)
Paris, Bibliothèque nationale de France

This family portrait served to further Henri IV's dynastic agenda, celebrating the birth of the new heir, Louis XIII. The focus of the image is the relationship between the king and his heir, who sits on the lap of his nurse. The king, surrounded by nobles and flanked on his right by his illegitimate son César, gazes at the young future king and extends his hand to him, cutting across the figure of the queen. Marie looks directly out at the viewer, her subordinate role made clear by the grouping of figures and their interrelationships.

LA REGENCE DE LA ROYNE ET SON PRVDENT GOVVERNEMENT DV ROY ET ENFANS DE FRANCE.

France qui recognois de quel soin ie fomente
Les sacrez Alcyons du Grand Henry ton Roy,
Si pour les conseruer tu veilles comme moy,
De tout contraire effort tu veincras la tormente.

Par l'Hymen sacre-sainct de mon frere et de moy
L'Espagne qui se voit a la France conjointe
Benira comme nous ceste alliance saincte
Quand ces peuples vnis croistront d'heur et de Roy.

Le Ciel qui me donna Mars indonte pour pere,
Cognoissant les dangers où ie fus par sa mort;
Voulut pour me tirer du lamentable sort,
Que la Royne m'aydast en Pallas et en mere.

60

LÉONARD GAULTIER
French, 1561–1641
The Regency of the Queen
and Her Prudent
Government of the King
and Children of France

1613
Engraving
233 × 308 mm (9⅞ × 12⅛ in.)
plate, 250 × 323 mm
(9⅞ × 12¾ in.) sheet
Lent by the Museum of Fine Arts,
Boston, Purchased from the Harriet
Otis Cruft Fund

Marie's success in international diplomacy as queen mother is lauded in this engraving. The previous year she had negotiated the betrothal of the young Dauphin and his future bride, Anne of Austria, daughter of King Philip III of Spain. The left side of the composition, dominated by Marie and her female children, is balanced by the predominately male side on the right with the Dauphin and Anne of Austria and the attendants of the king.

In England, unlike France, women could inherit the throne from their fathers, but the idea of an unmarried female ruler was anomalous. Queen Elizabeth I of England solved the problem through a variety of manipulations, designed to publicly promote her virginity as a source of her power. The queen, her court artists, and other supporters developed ways to project her power as a paragon of chastity, often melding these with traditional symbols of statecraft and imperialism (pl. 61).[11] Kings before her were often shown in robes of state, holding the insignia of their office, a scepter (or a sword) and an orb.[12] Official government documents, such as a Royal Grant embellished with a miniature after court artist Nicholas Hilliard, follow this kingly model and show Elizabeth enrobed, holding a scepter or a sword and an orb (pl. 62, detail, right).[13]

After Nicholas Hilliard, *Royal Grant showing initial* E *with miniature of Queen Elizabeth I,* 1571 (pl. 62, detail)

For other contexts, she is extolled in various ways as the virgin queen. Images employ a variety of symbols (sieve, column, pelican, phoenix, crescent moon) as well as the representation of the queen encased in garments encrusted with jewels to create a sense of her inaccessibility. These images appeared in paintings and prints, as well as in some of the medals, medallions, cameos (pls. 63, 64), and miniatures that Elizabeth gave to her favorites—and they replaced badges worn earlier representing the Virgin Mary, as the cult of the virgin queen took the place of the cult of the Virgin Mother. While the queen exerted control over her images in England, artists outside those boundaries could depart from portraying Elizabeth as the virgin queen, even showing her nude (pl. 65).

Crispin van de Passe's engraving of 1596 uses multiple symbols to convey an imperialist message (pl. 20). Elizabeth, sumptuously clad and holding scepter and orb, stands between two columns referring to the Pillars of Hercules, rocks that marked the limits of the ancient world. Elizabeth appropriated the symbol of the double columns from the Hapsburg emperor Charles V, who used it as his personal device to express Spain's extension to the Americas. The columns, as well as the ships symbolic of England's marine dominancy—recalling England's defeat of the Armada in 1588— refer to Elizabeth's ambitions for empire. Perched on one column is a bird symbolic of chastity—the phoenix, a mythical bird that rises from its own ashes after it has been consumed by fire. On the other column is a bird symbolic of charity and self-sacrifice and a reference to the queen as mother of her people—the pelican, a bird that pecks its chest to feed its own blood to its young.

The symbol of the sieve, attribute of the vestal virgin Tuccia, who carried water in a sieve as proof of her chastity, was a key way in which Elizabeth projected herself as a virgin queen and turned her chastity into a positive value. She was depicted holding a sieve in two series of paintings, one of 1579 and another of *c.* 1580–83. In the most complex example of this portrait type, the allegorical portrait now in Siena (fig. 30),[14] Elizabeth holds the sieve in one hand. Behind her at left is a column (representing fortitude, constancy, and chastity), with medallions inset into the column from the story of Dido and Aeneas. The latter spurned an entanglement with Dido for imperialist reasons—a reference to Elizabeth's own desire to show herself as bound by duty to remain chaste, rather than to marry. The inclusion of the globe asserts the imperialist ambitions

Fig. 30 Quentin Massys the Younger, *Portrait of Elizabeth I*, 1583, oil on canvas, 124.5 × 91.6 cm (49 × 36 in.), Siena, Pinacoteca Nazionale di Siena

of the virgin queen. Inscriptions on the surface of the painting refer to Elizabeth's abilities to discern the good from the bad and the imperial destiny made possible to the queen by rejecting love.

Beginning in the late 1580s, Elizabeth also conveyed her omnipotence and her chastity through the guise of Diana (also called Cynthia), the chaste goddess of the moon and of the hunt, who had dominion over waters, both seas and oceans.[15] Elizabeth is shown in numerous portraits wearing the attribute of Diana, a crescent moon, as a jewel in her hair, as in a miniature of c. 1595–1600 by Nicholas Hilliard (fig. 14). This miniature also shows Elizabeth as a young woman, in a timeless "Mask of Youth" developed by Hilliard in the mid-1590s to hide the queen's signs of age.[16] The bust format of the miniature shows her with the décolletage allowed to maidens, also alluding to her chastity.

Some portraits made explicit reference to the quasi-mystical idea in the popular political theory of this period of the king's two bodies, a notion going back to medieval times. In this concept the king (or queen) has both an institutional body (which never dies) and a physical body.[17] The concept was made apparent by her use of symbols of royal immortality such as the phoenix, in a famous medallion of 1574 (pl. 66). Its self-procreation made it a fitting symbol both for the legitimacy of Elizabeth's dynastic rule as well as her chastity.[18]

Aprill.

Ægloga Quarta.
ARGVMENT.

61

ANONYMOUS
16th century
Illustration to the *April Eclogue*, folio 11 in Edmund Spenser, *The Shepheardes Calendar*, London, Hugh Singleton, 1579

Woodcut
60 × 102 mm (2⅜ × 4 in.)
Harry Ransom Humanities Research Center, The University of Texas at Austin

Elizabeth I is shown as a regal figure holding official accoutrements of power— the scepter and orb. As the centermost of virginal figures— muses, graces, nymphs—she ushers in the Golden Age. In the text she is praised as Venus-Virgo, a figure symbolizing love and chastity.

After NICHOLAS
HILLIARD

English, c. 1547–1619

Royal Grant showing initial E with miniature of Queen Elizabeth I

1571

Tempera, gold leaf, and ink on vellum, attached by a cord to a bag of hessian cotton inscribed in ink, containing a broken wax seal

45.7 × 66 cm (18 × 26 in.) sheet, 13.9 cm (5½ in.) diam. bag

Stamford, Lincolnshire, The Burghley House Collection

This Royal Grant by which Sir William Cecil was created Lord Burghley in 1571 is embellished with a portrait of Queen Elizabeth in its initial miniature. This is a type of royal portraiture seen on formal documents. Like the English kings who preceded her, Elizabeth is shown iconically in full state regalia, wearing an ermine-lined robe of state, crowned, and holding scepter and orb. The Great Seal attached to the grant was at some point in its history smashed and sewn into a bag, which bears Lord Burghley's handwriting: 25 febr. 13. EI (25 February in the thirteenth year of Elizabeth's reign).

63

By or after GEORGE
GOWER
English, active 1540–1596
*Portrait of Queen
Elizabeth I*
c. 1588
Oil on canvas
101.4 × 97.5 cm (40 × 38¾ in.)
Private collection courtesy of Peter
Nahum At The Leicester Galleries

This portrait of Elizabeth—once
owned by King Charles I—
demonstrates the importance of
elaborate, even exaggerated, costume
in creating an imposing image of the
queen. The large lace ruff enframing
her face and the enormous sleeves of
her dress amplify her body, allowing
it to fill the canvas. Abundant jewels
and bows enhance the sense of the
queen's magnificence. The pearls
refer to her chastity and the feather
fan underscores her femininity.
Similar depictions of Elizabeth
emerged around the time of the
defeat of the Spanish Armada in
1588, some of the most famous of
which show the queen with her hand
on a globe.

ANONYMOUS

16th century

Portrait of Queen Elizabeth I

1580s

Agate cameo

23 × 14 mm (1 × ½ in.)

Collection of Christopher Foley

Elizabeth I gave cameos as gifts, and a number of portraits of her courtiers show them wearing cameo likenesses of her. This tiny agate cameo of Elizabeth I was probably intended for a ring or brooch. In this instance, the artist hollowed out the back of the agate behind the face of the cameo, giving it a translucent luminosity.

Die nacte waerheyt.
VICTE LINVS
DE MORT VA PARYS
CAPVCYNEN
DRAGHON
INQVISITION
HOL
O edele princesse lofbaer die hier reyn bloeme zijt verheuen
Van got vercoeren met uwen maechden seer schoone
Zijt altijt voersichtich oft ghij sult comen in sneuen
Dat fenijnich gebroetsel comt hem wt den dop verthone
Die eijeren van antechrijst en van belphegors sonen
Staen schoen gekipt in des moeders fnijdich harten
O godt mochten die ionghe breeken haer moeders crone
So bleuen dese landen te samen wt grooter smarten
Die gecroonde beest bedrijft veel booselijcke parten
Aen den moort van parijs heeftmen haer sien wencken
Soo mennich chris tenen haer bloet versmoert
En wilt den prins van oraengens doot gedencken
Doer den tijt metter waerheijt wort ons ghetoont.
Den schadelijcken nest ontdeckt met die brothen ghecroont.
Oich Nobel Prince and most famose flouer
Cossen of god wyth youer medes very ferre
By alwese Sercomspecte that you com not tho deuouer
That venomse brydyge showes him selfe out of the shell
The eges of Antycryst and belsebobes tower. feare.
and ferre taken in ther mothers hart of fier.
O god myght the youngonies brecke ther mouthers cronne and flouer.
So Remened thes landes to gether from deuouer.
The thry Cronned best dothe Ple mane venomose partes.
As by the morder of Parys wye haue Sinne him Shinne.
And mordered so mane a Cris ten bloud as bestes or Swyne.
Ther fore think vppon the Prince of Oryngs deth in tym.

65

PIETER VAN DER HEYDEN

Flemish, c. 1530–1575

Queen Elizabeth I and the Pope as Diana and Callisto

c. 1585

Engraving

255 × 341 mm (13½ × 10 in.)

London, The British Museum, Department of Prints and Drawings

In this propagandistic print Pieter van der Heyden freely drew from Titian's famous erotic paintings on the Ovidian story of Diana and Callisto. Callisto was one of Diana's nymphs, whom she discovered pregnant by Jupiter. Van der Heyden casts Queen Elizabeth I as Diana and Pope Gregory XIII as Callisto.

This satire was meant as a plea for Elizabeth's help in the struggle by the Low Countries to throw off the yoke of Catholic Spain.

66

ANONYMOUS

16th century

The Phoenix Medal, reverse of medal

c. 1574

Silver

45 × 41 mm (1¾ × 1⅝ in.)

London, The British Museum, Department of Coins and Medals

This famous medal is known as The Phoenix Medal because it shows one of Elizabeth I's favorite emblems, the phoenix. This mythical bird was believed to have risen from its ashes after it was consumed by fire. It was a perfect symbol for asserting both Elizabeth's claim to dynastic rule and her chastity.

Throughout history a sexually tempting, assertive, or conniving woman has been perceived as a threat to the social order. Among the most complex images of powerful women are those depicting characters from the Bible, ancient history, and myth whose stories involve seduction (pls. 67, 68, 70). Looking to Eve as the prototypical seductress, misogynist thinking going back to the Church fathers saw women as having a greater capacity for evil than men, primarily due to their potential to lead men into sin through their sexuality, beauty, and wiles. Stories of heroines such as Judith, who had seduced men for patriotic reasons, could lend themselves to visualizations in which the seduction or the danger to men was emphasized more than the service to the country.[19] In an engraving of c. 1550–80 by René Boyvin, Judith's nipples pressing through her garment and her look of longing eroticize the heroine and impute desire to her, as if the need for seduction conveniently corresponded with Judith's sexual intentions (pl. 69). The use of artifice to enhance beauty—as seen in Judith's elaborate braids in the same print—was considered dangerous to men and invoked the idea of vanity, showing beauty to be a power that was ephemeral. Hendrick Goltzius's small circular engraving of Judith uses direct confrontation with the viewer to emphasize the lethalness of her action (pl. 11). She holds the decapitated head of Holofernes toward the viewer, in a gesture recalling that in Benvenuto Cellini's *Perseus with the Head of Medusa*, a statue that stood in the Piazza della Signoria in Florence. Her hand illusionistically cuts across the inscription into the viewer's space, signalling both her prowess and the artist's own skill in illusionism.

This social threat was also expressed in images of male and female role reversal, with women dominating men, as in stories such as Aristotle and Phyllis (pl. 16), or Hercules and Omphale (pl. 44). As Natalie Davis has discussed, images of unruly women—women on top—have their roots in the ritual role reversal that characterized medieval social customs such as Carnival.[20] The notorious print series of the power of women, featuring figures from the Old Testament and secular legend in acts of treachery or deceit, have precedents in medieval imagery found, for example, in manuscript illumination or choirstall carvings. These motifs, as well as popular images of women beating or cuckolding their husbands, are more prevalent in the Northern countries, particularly beginning in the 1510s, in urban centers such as Leyden, Strasbourg, and Nuremberg.[21] Lucas van Leyden's two series were among the most famous.[22] His compositions were used for a series in the more costly medium of enamels for a more elevated audience, as in a set of oval plaques and a salt cellar by Pierre Reymond, all from the third quarter of the sixteenth century (pls. 71–77).[23] Dirck Volkertsz. Coornhert's series of six images of the *Power of Women* (figs. 31, 32 and pls. 28, 37, 38, 78), after designs by Maarten van Heemskerck, is an especially virulent example of the misogynist series. Here Eve, Lot's daughters, Jael, Delilah, Judith, and the Queen of Sheba are represented as powerful, muscular females. Their androgyny and the violence of their actions give a vivid sense of their danger.

Seductress stories provided an opportunity for nudity, whether justified by the story or not. Nudity is of course called for by the story of the temptation of Adam by Eve (pl. 7). But in cases in which nudity is not justified *textually*, a heroine can be construed

Fig. 31 Dirck Volkertsz. Coornhert, after Maarten van Heemskerck, *Eve Offering Adam the Forbidden Fruit*, from *The Power of Women*, a set of six, 1551, engraving and etching, 248 × 195 mm (9¾ × 7⅝ in.), Amsterdam, Rijksmuseum

Fig. 32 Dirck Volkertsz. Coornhert, after Maarten van Heemskerck, *Lot and His Daughters*, from *The Power of Women*, a set of six, 1551, engraving and etching, 249 × 197 mm (9¾ × 7¾ in.), Vienna, Graphische Sammlung Albertina

visually as a seductress. The Beham brothers, Barthel and Hans Sebald, active in Germany in the 1540s and 1550s, specialized in small-scale images extracted from a narrative context so as to better concentrate on the female form.[24] In one of these scenes (shown here in a copy by Jerome Wierix), Judith is depicted nude, while her handmaiden wears form-revealing drapery. Judith holds the head of Holofernes in one hand and a sword in the other, its blade held between her legs and its handle placed suggestively in front of her handmaiden's pubic area[25] (pl. 27). In another print a nude Judith fondles Holofernes's beard (pl. 79).

Images of Venus embody seduction and provide rich opportunities for developing implications of the gaze (pl. 80). Simon Vouet's painting of the *Toilette of Venus* intertwines concepts of desire, vanity, and deception (pl. 26). Showing Venus partially nude—and arrayed for the viewer—draws attention to her erotic aspects, which are countered yet enhanced by the act of covering her body. Without the element of the mirror the viewer's pleasure at this figure would be voyeuristic, yet this attribute, by catching the viewer's eye through Venus's direct gaze, implicates the spectator. The mirror symbolizes both vanity, in Venus's act of looking at herself, and deception—that the mirror does not really show the world as it is and that there is the capacity for deception in love.[26]

67
Follower of
BERNARDINO LUINI
Italian, c. 1480–1532
Salome with the Head of
St. John the Baptist

16th century
Oil on canvas
46.6 × 59.7 cm (18½ × 23½ in.)
The Cleveland Museum of Art,
Holden Collection

This work, based on a painting by Bernardino Luini now in the Uffizi Gallery, presents a cast of characters from the New Testament story of Salome—the heroine, her handmaiden (or mother, Herodias), the head of St. John the Baptist, and the executioner of the saint. The juxtaposition of Salome's young, comely face with that of the older woman stresses the fleeting aspect of beauty—and of female power derived from it. Inasmuch as Salome's beauty—and Herod's lust for her—brought about St. John the Baptist's decapitation, the image conveys the treachery of female allure.

68

LUCAS VAN LEYDEN
Dutch, c. 1494–1533

Salome taking the Head of St. John the Baptist to Herodias, from the series The Small Power of Women

c. 1517
Woodcut
244 × 175 mm (9⅝ × 6⅞ in.)
block, 246 × 179 mm (9¾ × 7 in.)
sheet
Lent by the Museum of Fine Arts, Boston, Gift of Mrs. Lydia Evans Tunnard in memory of W.G. Russell Allen

Lucas van Leyden's two print series of the Power of Women influenced the subsequent development of the theme, in that they were used as models for later series. In this image, the artist presents the complicity of Herodias and her daughter in the martyrdom of St. John the Baptist, while stressing Salome's allure with her suggestive pose.

69

RENÉ BOYVIN
French, c. 1530?–1625?
After GIOVANNI
BATTISTA DI JACOPO,
called ROSSO
FIORENTINO
Italian, 1494–1540
**Judith with the Head of
Holofernes**

c. 1550–80
Engraving
180 × 130 mm (7⅛ × 5⅛ in.)
Paris, Bibliothèque nationale de
France

Chiefly a reproductive engraver,
René Boyvin helped disseminate
the works of artists of the
Fontainebleau school. This print,
showing Judith with the head of
Holofernes displayed on a ledge,
is based on a design by Rosso
Fiorentino. Judith is an elegant,
elaborately coiffed beauty. Her
nipples pressing through her
drapery and her look of longing
eroticize the heroine.

70

JAKOB BINCK
German, 1500–1569
or GIOVANNI JACOPO
CARAGLIO
Italian, *c.* 1500/05–1565
After GIOVANNI
BATTISTA DI JACOPO,
called ROSSO
FIORENTINO
Italian, 1494–1540
Mars and Venus

c. 1530–40
Engraving
419 × 335 mm (16½ × 13¼ in.)
Ann Arbor, University of Michigan
Museum of Art, 1985

Elaborating on stories from
several classical texts, Binck's
engraving after Rosso depicts a
scene in which Mars and Venus
are being prepared for
lovemaking. Venus sits on her
bed, being undressed by the
Three Graces, while Mars
receives help from various putti.
The focus of the satire is Mars's
alarm, indicated by his fearful
expression and shrinking pose.
Stripped of his armor, with
which the amoretti now play,
Mars now has to demonstrate his
virile capacity in another arena.
Perhaps Venus has effectively
unmanned Mars; or perhaps it is
that his true endowment, or lack
thereof, has been exposed.

71

PIERRE REYMOND

French, c. 1513–after 1584

Solomon Turns to Idolatry, from The Power of Women, a set of six

Third quarter of the 16th century

Painted enamel

292 × 235 mm (11⅝ × 9½ in.)

Baltimore, The Walters Art Museum

72

PIERRE REYMOND

French, c. 1513–after 1584

Jael Kills Sisera, from The Power of Women, a set of six

Third quarter of the 16th century

Painted enamel

292 × 237 mm (11⅝ × 9⅜ in.)

Baltimore, The Walters Art Museum

73

PIERRE REYMOND
French, c. 1513–after 1584

Adam and Eve, from
The Power of Women,
a set of six

Third quarter of the 16th century
Painted enamel
279 × 222 mm (11 × 8¾ in.)
London, Victoria and Albert Museum

74

PIERRE REYMOND

French, *c.* 1513–after 1584

*Lot and His Daughters,
from The Power of
Women, a set of six*

Third quarter of the 16th century
Painted enamel
279 × 222 mm (11 × 8¾ in.)
London, Victoria and Albert Museum

75

PIERRE REYMOND

French, *c.* 1513–after 1584

*Samson and Delilah,
from The Power of
Women, a set of six*

Third quarter of the 16th century
Painted enamel
279 × 222 mm (11 × 8¾ in.)
London, Victoria and Albert Museum

PIERRE REYMOND
French, c. 1513–after 1584
Judith and Holophernes,
from The Power of
Women, a set of six

Third quarter of the 16th century
Painted enamel
279 × 229 mm (11 × 9 in.)
London, Victoria and Albert Museum

The power of women was a
misogynistic theme that satirized
famous women from ancient and
biblical history who overpowered
men through their sexual allure.
The essential message was a
warning about female power—
that women are inherently
deceitful, and that men, even the
strongest and most intelligent,
are helpless before their charms.
Reymond's plaques attest to the
dissemination of this theme into
a more rarefied medium, the
enamel, which would have been
intended for a wealthier social
milieu than the more broadly
accessible print.

77

PIERRE REYMOND
French, *c.* 1513–after 1584
Hexagonal salt cellar with the Power of Women (Masculine Weakness), showing scenes of *The Original Sin, Solomon and the Queen of Sheba, Jael and Sisera, The Fable of Virgil, Samson and Delilah, The Lay of Aristotle*

Mid-16th century
Painted enamel
Height 75 × diam. 93 mm
(height 2⅞ × diam. 3⅝ in.)
Paris, Musée du Louvre, Département des Objets d'art

This salt cellar, by Pierre Reymond, one of the foremost French enamelists of the Renaissance, is a good example of the serial presentation of power of women subjects. Comparison among the stories from ancient and biblical history serves to reinforce the message of women's deceitfulness and men's fallibility. The appearance of the topos in this object of everyday use, however, suggests a less-than-serious approach to the theme: power of women subjects were commonly used in satires of marriage.

78

DIRCK VOLKERTSZ. COORNHERT
Dutch, 1522–1590
After MAARTEN VAN HEEMSKERCK
Dutch, 1498–1574
Solomon's Idolatry, from *The Power of Women*, a set of six

1551
Engraving and etching
248 × 195 mm (9¾ × 7¾ in.)
Lent by The Metropolitan Museum of Art, New York, Rogers Fund, 1966

HANS SEBALD BEHAM
German, 1500–1550
After BARTHEL BEHAM
German, 1502–1540
Judith Seated in an Arch

1547
Engraving
75 × 50 mm (3 × 2 in.)
Ann Arbor, University of Michigan
Museum of Art, The W. Hawkins
Ferry Fund, 1998

Beham's print eliminates nearly
all details of the biblical
narrative, isolating Judith and
the decapitated head of
Holofernes in a moment of
intimacy. Casting a gentle gaze
down at his head, Judith caresses
it with her right hand. A sensual
interpretation of the story is
emphasized through Judith's
classically inspired nudity, and
by details such as the touch of
Holofernes's beard to Judith's
thigh. The upright sword in her
left hand seems to indicate, in
contrast to the image's dominant
note of feminine voluptuousness,
the virile masculine resolve that
led her to triumph over her
powerful enemy.

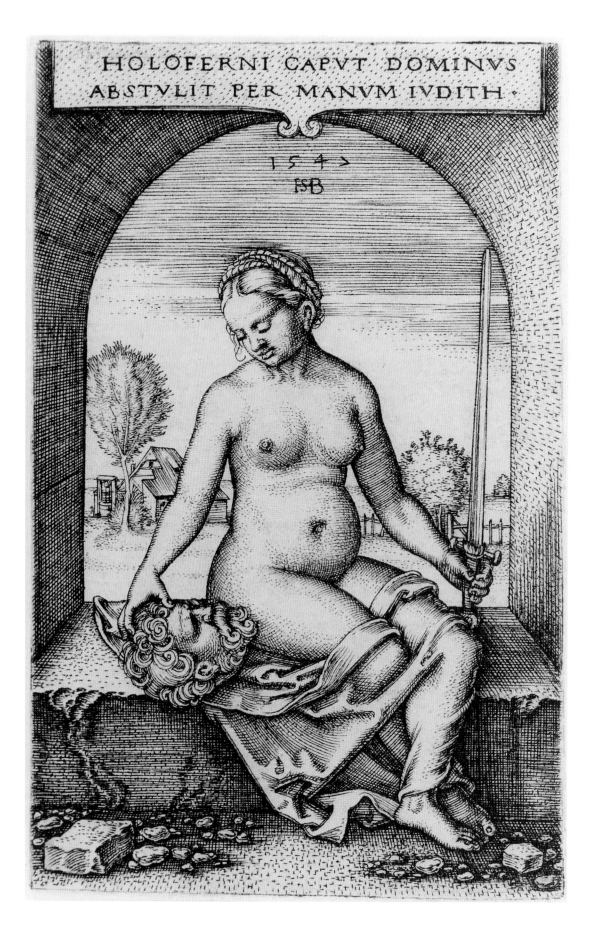

80

GUIDO RENI
Italian, 1575–1642
Venus and Cupid

c. 1626

Oil on canvas

280 × 157 cm (89¾ × 61¾ in.)
Toledo, Toledo Museum of Art,
Purchased with funds from the
Libbey Endowment, Gift of Edward
Drummond Libbey

In Guido Reni's painting Venus's
comely form is discernible
beneath gossamer-thin drapery.
The modeling of her flesh is
achieved by subtle tonal shifts.
The figure of Venus often
provides an opportunity for the
artist to engage in a show of skill
so as to seduce the spectator.

Fig. 33 Eustache Le Sueur, *Camma Offers the Poisoned Wedding Cup to Synorix in the Temple to Diana,* c. 1644, oil on canvas, 171.8 × 125.7 cm (67⅝ × 49½ in.), Museum of Fine Arts, Boston, M. Theresa B. Hopkins Fund, 48.16

IV. THE HEROINE

The phenomenon of women ruling seems to have encouraged artists to take up themes of strong women acting heroically. They did so in painting cycles or book illustrations of famous women from the past known as "galleries of strong women." Many of the illustrated treatises of the time showing heroines were dedicated to rulers such as Marie de' Medici and Anne of Austria. But rather than show actual women of their own times acting heroically, Renaissance and Baroque artists turned to the Old Testament, classical history, and the remote and recent past for prototypes. This section looks at the heroine (or heroic woman), as seen in images of valiant women viewed positively, triumphing as females in a male world.[27]

Yet even images of heroic women can contain layers of ambiguity. For example, Judith, whose role as a dangerous temptress is sometimes stressed, as we have seen, at other times is shown heroically (pl. 81). In a painting by Massimo Stanzione showing Judith with her handmaiden, she is given a pose reminiscent of the famous classical sculpture, the Apollo Belvedere, which accords her dignity and underlines the nobility of her deed (fig. 6). Cornelis Galle, in his copy after Rubens, who was inspired by Caravaggio's famous painting of Judith killing Holofernes, features a robust, capable young woman, though the image does have erotic undertones, such as the thrusting of Judith's fingers into Holofernes's mouth (pl. 82).[28]

The paradox of women exercising virtues outside the female norm becomes an important concept in the sixteenth and early seventeenth centuries and informs the ideal of the *femme forte*, or strong woman.[29] The *femme forte* possessed not only the traditional masculine virtue of *fortitudo*—a constellation of virtues such as liberality, magnanimity, and constancy—but also chastity, and writers disagreed as to whether chastity was actually a heroic virtue like courage. The *femme forte* not only embodied this enlarged gamut of virtues, but she also possessed beauty as a positive value.[30] In the early seventeenth century various writers stress the equality of men and women. Jacques Du Bosc's *La femme héroïque*, one of the most important feminist works of the seventeenth century, mounts the argument that women possess the same virtues as men.[31] Eight pairs of famous women and men from biblical and ancient history are discussed, their characters and accomplishments compared. His women excel in "masculine" virtues, while his men do better than women in "female" virtues. The illustrations of the heroines and heroes, which open on facing pages, often make a point of their equality through formal means, in the repetition of gestures, or in mirrored compositions (pls. 8, 9, 10).

Eustache Le Sueur's painting of Camma represents a heroine from ancient history who often figured in compendiums of illustrious women (fig. 33).[32] The painting is a vivid illustration of the possibilities that chastity offered to the *femme forte* for self-assertion. The princess and priestess Camma sacrificed her own life in order to avenge the death of her husband, Sinatus. In order to deceive his murderer, Synorix, she agreed to marry him, and then proceeded to poison him and herself during their wedding ceremony. Le Sueur's painting captures the most dramatic moment of the story, when Camma has already ingested the poisoned drink and offers it to Synorix. The ceremony took place in the temple of Diana, goddess of chastity, where Camma was a priestess. The prominent position given to the statue of Diana in the painting symbolizes Camma's virtue and loyalty to her husband.

81

ALBRECHT DÜRER
German, 1471–1528

The Annunciation, from The Life of the Virgin

c. 1503
Woodcut
295 × 212 mm (11⅝ in. × 8⅜ in.)
Ann Arbor, University of Michigan
Museum of Art, Gift of the Friends
of the Museum in memory of Helen
B. Hall, Curator Emeritus, 1992

Dürer has depicted a relief of
Judith holding the head of
Holofernes in the uppermost
roundel of his Annunciation,
and has directed the viewer's eye
to this ostensibly peripheral
location with his use of
perspective and the framing arch.
The story of Judith was
interpreted in the sixteenth
century as a prefiguration of the
Virgin's triumph over the Devil,
who appears in this scene
chained beneath the stairs.

82

CORNELIS GALLE THE
ELDER
Flemish, 1576–1650
After PETER PAUL
RUBENS
Flemish, 1577–1640
*Judith Beheading
Holofernes*

c. 1610
Engraving
550 × 380 mm (21⅝ × 15 in.)
Lent by The Metropolitan Museum
of Art, New York, The Elisha
Whittelsey Collection, The Elisha
Whittelsey Fund, 1951

This engraving was the first
reproductive print commissioned
by Rubens. Integrating elements
from Adam Elsheimer's and
Caravaggio's paintings of the
same theme, Rubens's work is
striking in its graphic portrayal
of the subject. Judith deftly slices
through the neck of the writhing
Holofernes, seemingly
unperturbed by spurting blood
or by the fact that her fingers
have slipped into his screaming
mouth. Holofernes's powerful,
muscular body, which recalls
classical sculpture such as the
famous *Laocöon*, serves to further
emphasize Judith's divinely
ordained prowess.

Cedite Romani ductores, cedite Graij: Veſtra fuit magna victoria parta virùm vi,   Barbarus vnius dextrâ cadit Induperator,
Obſtruxit veſtris femina luminibus.   Et ceſſit laudis pars bona militibus;   Defendit patriæ perniciem vna manus.

Clariſſ. et amiciſsimo viro D. IOANNI WOVERIO paginam hanc auspicalem primumque ſuorum operum
typis æneis expreſſum PETRVS PAVLLVS RVBENIVS promiſſi von olim Veronæ a se facti memor DAT DICAT.

The figure of the warrior woman was a multivalent symbol, used to depict women who distinguished themselves in traditional "male" qualities of bravery and courage, as well as chastity. Famous warrior women from the past were depicted, such as Zenobia, Queen of Palmyra, Joan of Arc, and Clorinda from Tasso's *La Gerusalemme Liberata* (pls. 13, 83, 84), serving, perhaps, to inspire women to acts of valor. The image of the warrior was above all a symbol of the woman who had stepped out of her traditional role into a sphere of action.

The early modern period in Europe, marked by frequent wars, saw the rise of images of fighting women. This reflected reality, because many noblewomen were forced to defend their lands and go into battle.[33] Some of these women had themselves depicted armed for battle. Madame de Saint-Baslemont, warrior and poet from the 1630s and 1640s, had herself portrayed in full battle gear on horseback (not riding sidesaddle) with her lands in the background.[34] In the time of the civil wars known as the Frondes (1648–1653), in which nobles rose up against the state, members of the highest nobility took part in battle. One of the most famous of these was the self-styled Amazon, the celebrated Mademoiselle de Montpensier (known as "La Grande Mademoiselle"), Anne Marie Louise, Duchess of Orléans, granddaughter of Marie de' Medici, who led the victorious siege of Orléans.[35] A member of the School of Pierre Mignard painted her portrait (fig. 34) and those of other noble ladies dressed like Amazons, after a formulaic pattern suggesting a full-blown fashion.

Female rulers typically presented themselves as capable of warfare or responsible for successes in war allegorically. Allegorizations of war or of peacetime, when arts and learning could flourish, were important in early modern Europe; those in the court of Rudolph II of Prague, for example, were painted to glorify his endeavors (pls. 86, 87). A portrait medal of Margaret of Austria, Duchess of Parma made during her regency (1559–67) represents on its reverse an allegory of war and peace (pl. 85). The figure holding a sword and the olive branch of peace is to be identified as Margaret, who as governor-general of the Netherlands had quelled insurrections. Her court advisor evolved this manner of presenting her, and she had copies send to dignitaries, including the pope.[36]

In the great painting cycle glorifying the life of Marie de' Medici, which she commissioned from Peter Paul Rubens to decorate the Palais du Luxembourg (now at the Musée du Louvre), Rubens represented her dressed in armor as the Roman goddess Minerva Victrix. This aspect of Minerva refers to military triumph, and the goddess is traditionally represented standing amid armor and holding a statue of Victory. This image of Marie de' Medici (shown here in a reproductive engraving, pl. 22) functioned both as a portrait and as a testimony to her ability to guide the country during her regency. With a statue of Victory in one hand and a scepter in the other, she stands on a battlefield amid cannons, trampling armor. She valorizes herself as a female ruler with these masculine accoutrements of war, as well as with the bared breast of an Amazon (a member of an ancient legendary tribe of warrior women who set themselves apart from men, famously cutting off their right breasts to help them shoot arrows).[37]

Fig. 34 School of Pierre Mignard, *Anne Marie Louise d'Orléans, "La Grande Mademoiselle,"* c. 1664, oil on canvas, 130 × 98 cm (51⅛ × 38½ in.), Stockholm, Nationalmuseum, Collection of Gripsholm Castle, NMGrh 1169

83

Attributed to
PETER PAUL RUBENS
Flemish, 1577–1640
Joan of Arc

c. 1618–20
Oil on canvas
181.8 × 116.3 cm (71½ × 45¾ in.)
Raleigh, North Carolina Museum of
Art, Raleigh, Purchased with funds
from the State of North Carolina and
the North Carolina Art Society,
Robert F. Phifer Bequest

Joan of Arc was frequently
included in the popular
illustrated series of *femme fortes*
(strong women), heroic women
from mythology and history.
Full-size representations of her
as in this painting were
uncommon, however. The figure
of the heroine, kneeling in
prayer before a crucifix, was
probably modeled after prints
of a sculptural monument to
the saint in Orléans. This image
seems to convey a mixed message
about the heroine, with the
masculinity of the full suit of
armor offset by her flowing
golden Rubenesque locks, and
her humble, almost demure
piety.

LAURENT DE LA HYRE
French, 1606–1656

*Tancred and Clorinda,
a scene from Torquato
Tasso, La Gerusalemme
Liberata*

Before 1630
Black and white chalk
292 × 400 mm (11½ × 15¾ in.)
Ann Arbor, University of Michigan
Museum of Art, Purchased from the
Estate of Edward Sonnenschein,
1970

This drawing is one from a
group of twelve studies by
La Hyre depicting scenes from
Tasso's celebrated crusader story,
La Gerusalemme liberata (Jerusalem
delivered). This drawing
represents an episode involving
the Christian knight Tancred
and the female warrior Clorinda.
The drawing depicts the moment
when Tancred discovers the
identity of his adversary after
having killed her in combat.
Clorinda was one of the favorite
warrior women of the
Renaissance and Baroque periods.

85

JACQUES
JONGHELINCK
(JONGELING)
Flemish, 1530–1606

Margaret of Austria,
Duchess of Parma,
as an allegorical figure
in classical garments,
reverse of medal

1559–67
Cast silver
595 mm (2⅜ in.) diam.
Brussels, Royal Library of Belgium,
Coins and Medals

Margaret of Austria, Duchess of
Parma, was asked by Philip II to
become governor-general of the
Netherlands in 1559. This
medal shows on its obverse a
profile portrait of Margaret, and
on its reverse an allegory of war
and peace. The figure holding
a sword and palm and olive
branches is to be identified as
Margaret herself. Her rule was
distinguished by her attempts
to bring insurrections under
control.

JAN MULLER
Dutch, 1571–1628

After BARTHOLOMÄUS
SPRANGER
Flemish, 1546–1611

Bellona Leading the Armies of the Emperor Against the Turks

1600
Engraving
704 × 510 mm (27¾ × 20 in.)
Lent by The Minneapolis Institute of
Arts, The Ethel Morrison Van Derlip
Fund

The Turkish wars (1593–1606)
were one of the greatest threats
to Emperor Rudolf II's rule.
Here, Bellona, the goddess of
war, leads the emperor's troops
in battle. A winged figure in the
top left seems ready to bestow a
palm frond and laurel wreath,
traditional symbols of victory,
on the imperial forces. Many
imperial allegories of this period
present the emperor as a
defender of Christian Europe
against the Turkish barbarians.
The print was undoubtedly
intended to promote the
emperor's cause against
the Turks.

AEGIDIUS SADELER
Flemish, 1570–1629

After BARTHOLOMÄUS
SPRANGER
Flemish, 1546–1611

The Triumph of Wisdom over Ignorance

c. 1600
Engraving
508 × 358 mm (20 × 14⅛ in.)
Chapel Hill, Ackland Art Museum,
The University of North Carolina at
Chapel Hill, Ackland Fund

Aegidius Sadeler held the post of imperial engraver under Holy Roman Emperor Rudolf II in Prague. Minerva, the goddess of wisdom and the arts, is shown subjugating the figure of Ignorance, and is surrounded by personifications of the arts. Minerva appears frequently in allegories produced in Rudolf's court, a reference to Rudolf's extensive patronage of the arts. Although the exact meaning of this sophisticated allegory is debated, it is possible that the print's intended message was similar to that of other Rudolfine allegories that present the emperor as protector of the arts and civilization.

B. Spranger inuent.
Eg. Sadeler fecit.

Non datur, ex imis venerer, ut INSCIVS ARTES, &c INSCIVS NON HONORABITur. Sed datur, ut spreta iaceat calcatus ab ARTE
Sedne eas quærens noscere gestit AMOR. INSCIVS, et solido cassus honore ruat.

Depicting a ruler as an Olympian god or goddess accorded with the idea at this time that kings and queens were quasi-divine. Artists and patrons looked to classical mythology for inspiration in aggrandizing rulers in royal portraits and ceremonies proclaiming their godly qualities. Rulers were given the attributes of gods and goddesses, or were represented in complex allegories with a cast of mythological figures (pl. 88).

The reign of Henri IV and Marie de' Medici was particularly rich in mythological symbols, and the choice of celestial deities relates to gendered roles. In a pair of salt cellars bearing their portraits, attributed to the enamelist Jean de Court, the foot of each vessel shows a chariot with a different divinity (pls. 90, 91). Festivities and ceremonial entries featuring gods in chariots seem referenced here. Marie's vessel shows a chariot drawn by Diana, who is associated not only with chastity but also with childbirth,[38] while Henri's chariot is drawn by Venus, goddess of love. Is this simply an assertion of the importance of love in the royal marriage, or a possible reference to the double standard—the fact that it was acceptable for men, even expected of male rulers, to have numerous affairs?

A small sculpture of Marie in the guise of Juno, the chief Roman goddess, is part of a pair created c. 1600 on the occasion of her wedding to Henri IV, who was depicted as Jupiter, the supreme Roman deity (pl. 89). As protectress of marriage and childbirth, Juno was appropriate to the roles of wife and mother for a female consort.[39] As a regent Marie had herself depicted again as Juno, this time seated on a rainbow, a reference to her role as bringer of peace (the rainbow was a sign of God's covenant with Noah after the flood) (pl. 92). Before her, Catherine de' Medici had used the rainbow as her personal device, and Elizabeth I was depicted with this attribute in the Rainbow portrait.[40]

Medalists frequently represented Henri IV and Marie de' Medici as gods. They are depicted in the guise of Mars and Minerva in medals with dynastic messages, for example, in one celebrating the birth of the Dauphin (pl. 41) and in another celebrating their love, which produces offspring (pl. 93).[41] After Marie became regent she had herself depicted as Minerva, charged with wisely guiding the young Louis XIII (pl. 95).[42] To mark her leadership, she had herself depicted during her regency in the guise of Cybele (an ancient mother goddess who ruled over nature) (pl. 94). A medal depicts her as Cybele steering the ship of state, however a painting in Rubens's cycle (shown here in a reproductive engraving) depicts her handing the rudder to her son (pls. 96, 97).[43] Another painting in Rubens's cycle, *The Felicity of the Regency*, shows the diademed queen at her most regal as Astraea (the virgin goddess identified with justice), with a pair of scales in her right hand (pl. 23). She is attended in this commemoration of the golden age of her regency by other divine figures, including Minerva, Saturn, and Abundance.[44]

Christina of Sweden had herself represented in the guise of different deities. A small painting on the case of an ornamental clock (c. 1646) shows her as Diana, accompanied by nymphs; the emphasis here is on her chastity.[45] An allusion to the intellectual qualities of the "Minerva of the North," as Christina was known throughout Europe, is made in a reproductive print of 1649 by Jeremias Falck (pl. 98). This engraving shows her as a sculptural bust of Minerva, wearing a laurel-wreathed helmet, and accompanied by

Fig. 35 Anthony van Dyck, *Sir George Villiers and Lady Katherine Manners as Adonis and Venus*, late 1620–early 1621, oil on canvas, 223.5 × 160 cm (88 × 63 in.), private collection

the goddess's symbols of learning and wisdom, books and an owl.[46] She is linked to Hercules in the illustrated title page of the second volume of B. P. von Chemnitz's history of the Swedish armies in Germany (1653), engraved by Falck after a design by Sébastien Bourdon. This shows her receiving the god's club from the hands of her deceased father, Gustav II Adolf (pl. 48).[47]

Mythification was not limited to royalty, but became a fashion among the nobility as well. A portrait by Anthony van Dyck of Sir George Villiers and Lady Katherine Manners as Adonis and Venus shows them both partially draped after depictions of classical figures (fig. 35).[48] Lady Manners adopts the *Venus pudica* pose, which evokes both modesty and sensuality, both hiding and calling attention to erogenous zones.

While we cannot attempt to adduce from the material in this exhibition every sort of visual stratagem that was used in female imagery of this period, those that tend to recur relate to broad concerns of expectations about gender. Through the use of symbols, myths, references to the Bible, literature, and history, and through a variety of ways of presenting the female body, artists translated patrons' desires and came up with new ways to suggest the power of women and its limitations.

88

ALEXIS LOIR
French, 1640–1713

After JEAN-MARC
NATTIER
French, 1685–1766

After PETER PAUL
RUBENS
Flemish, 1577–1640

**The Education of the
Queen**

c. 1704–08
Engraving
445 × 337 mm (17½ × 13¼ in.)
Düsseldorf, Kunstmuseum
Düsseldorf, Graphische Sammlung

This reproductive engraving after
a painting in Rubens's cycle on
the life of Marie de' Medici
shows the young Marie,
accompanied by the three graces.
Minerva instructs Marie as a
young man plays a *viola da
gamba*. A sculptural bust, tools
of painting and sculpture, and
musical instruments refer to the
arts, which were part of Marie's
education.

Rubens pinxit.   J. M. Nattier delin   Loir Sculpsit.

L'Education de la Reine.

Minerve enseigne à la Reine les premiers élemens des sciences. Les Graces et l'harmonie accompagne cette Deesse,
pour assaisonner tout ce qui entre dans l'esprit de la jeune Princesse. Mercure descend du Ciel pour lui faire part
de son Eloquence, & la fontaine castalide est icy le simbole de la Poësie. Sur le devant du Tableau sont quelques instru-
mens des Arts Liberaux que la Reine a toujours aimez & protegez, & entr'autres la Peinture, la Sculpture, & la Musique.

A Paris chez le S.r Nattier, peintre de l'Academie Royale rüe Fromenteau.   Avec Privilege du Roy.

89

Attributed to

MATTHIEU JACQUET
French, 1545?–1611
Marie de' Medici as Juno

c. 1600?
Bronze
Height 48.5 × width 30 cm
(height 19⅛ × width 11⅞ in.)
Baltimore, The Walters Art Museum

Jacquet's *Marie de' Medici as Juno*,
with her attribute the peacock,
is the pendant to a statuette of
Henri IV as Jupiter. These
allegorical representations of the
royal pair as a mythological
couple were probably produced
shortly after Henri and Marie
were married in 1600, a union
that was viewed as ushering in a
golden age. The pose and figure
type of Marie are intended to call
to mind classical sculpture,
although the work does not seem
to be modeled after any
particular antique prototype.

90

Attributed to

JEAN DE COURT

French, active 1572–1585

Portrait of Henri IV and The Triumph of Venus, salt cellar

Early 17th century

Enamel

Height 80 × diam. 90 mm
(height 3⅛ × diam. 3½ in.)

Angers, Musées d'Angers

91

Attributed to

JEAN DE COURT

French, active 1572–1585

Portrait of Marie de' Medici and The Triumph of Diana, salt cellar

Early 17th century

Enamel

Height 80 × diam. 90 mm
(height 3⅛ × diam. 3½ in.)

Angers, Musées d'Angers

The subjects of these portraits depicted on this pair of salt cellars have been identified as Henri IV and Marie de' Medici. The foot of each vessel shows a chariot with a different divinity. Marie's vessel is decorated with a chariot driven by Diana, associated with both chastity and childbirth. Henri's chariot is drawn by Venus, goddess of love.

92

NICOLAS BRIOT

French, 1605–1646

Marie de' Medici as Juno on a rainbow with the fleur-de-lis of France, reverse of medal

1613
Struck silver
52 mm (2⅛ in.) diam.
Paris, Bibliothèque nationale de France

Juno was one of Marie de' Medici's preferred deities, both before and during her regency. On this medal she is shown as Juno holding her peacock and seated on a rainbow, which refers to her role as peacemaker. Catherine de' Medici and Elizabeth I also used the rainbow as a similar device.

93

Attributed to
PHILIPPE DANFRIE
THE YOUNGER
French, c. 1572–1604
*Henri IV as Mars and
Marie de' Medici as
Minerva, reverse of
medal*

1604
Struck silver
56 mm (2¼ in.) diam.
Los Angeles, Los Angeles County
Museum of Art

On the reverse of this medal
attributed to Philippe Danfrie
the Younger, Henri IV, holding
a scepter, and Marie de' Medici,
bearing a cornucopia, are shown
seated. They hold their hands
over an altar from which flames
arise. The inscription MAIESTAS
MAIOR AB IGNE, "Majesty is
increased from the flame," may
refer to their love, which
produces offspring.

94

GUILLAUME DUPRÉ
French, c. 1576–1643
*Marie de' Medici as
mother of the gods,
reverse of medal*

1624
Bronze
54 mm (2⅛ in.) diam.
National Gallery of Art, Washington,
Samuel H. Kress Collection

This medal shows on its reverse
Marie de' Medici in the guise of
Cybele. She is the centermost
of several regal, standing deities.
This medal is a vivid example of
Marie's strategy of portraying
herself as a goddess in order to
proclaim her semi-divine power.

GUILLAUME DUPRÉ
French, c. 1576–1643

Louis XIII as Apollo and Marie de' Medici as Minerva, reverse of medal

1611
Cast silver
49 mm (2 in.) diam.
London, The British Museum,
Department of Coins and Medals

This medal celebrates the assumption of power by Marie de' Medici as regent. To convey that it is she who brings peace and makes war, she is shown on the reverse as Minerva, holding an olive branch and a thunderbolt, and seated before a trophy. The young king, Louis XIII, shown as Apollo, looks up to her as tutelary, as is emphasized by the inscription, which reads, translated, "The King grows up under the guidance of Minerva."

96

GUILLAUME DUPRÉ

French, c. 1576–1643

Marie de' Medici as Cybele, reverse of medal

1615
Cast bronze
62 mm (2½ in.) diam.
London, Victoria and Albert Museum
(Salting Bequest)
(Illustration: The Metropolitan
Museum of Art, New York)

During her regency Marie de' Medici had herself represented as Cybele, the mother goddess who ruled over nature. Her elevation to the status of a goddess is stressed by the inscription SERVANDO DEA FACTA DEOS, "To save the gods she became a goddess." Here she wears Cybele's mural crown and steers the ship of state through a storm. Whereas in this medal she is shown at the helm, in Rubens's later painting in his cycle of her life, she has given the tiller to her son, Louis XIII.

97

ANTOINE TROUVAIN

French, 1656–1708

After JEAN-BAPTISTE NATTIER

French, 1678–1726

After PETER PAUL RUBENS

Flemish, 1577–1640

The Majority of Louis XIII

c. 1704–08
Engraving
442 × 339 mm
(17⅜ × 13⅜ in.)
Washington, Smithsonian Institution
National Museum of American
History, Behring Center

Trouvain's engraving of Rubens's painting recalls an image that appears on the reverse of a medal of 1615 by Guillaume Dupré in which Marie, as Cybele, steers the ship of state through a violent storm. In Rubens's painting, and in Trouvain's engraving of Louis's majority, the point at which Louis assumed the throne from his mother, a significant alteration has been made: it is Louis XIII who steers the ship, while his mother, Marie, gestures to the helm, either in guidance or acknowledging Louis's control.

La Majorite du Roy Louis XIII.

JEREMIAS FALCK
Polish, c. 1610

After DAVID BECK
Dutch, c. 1621–1656

and ERASMUS
QUELLINUS
Flemish, 1607–1678

*Christina of Sweden as
Minerva*

1649
Engraving
350 × 224 mm (13⅞ × 9 in.)
Düsseldorf, Kunstmuseum
Düsseldorf, Graphische Sammlung
Ann Arbor and Memphis only

Queen Christina of Sweden was
frequently represented as
Minerva during her reign. As
the goddess of the arts, wisdom,
and just war, representations of
Minerva could carry various and
multiple connotations. Here,
attributes associated with
wisdom and peace—the owl,
a stack of books, and an olive
branch—surround the marble
bust of Christina, referring to
Christina's reputation for great
learnedness.

NOTES

1 See Langedijk 1981, vol. I, pp. 98–100, 694–97, nos. 9–10; Langdon 1992, vol. I, pp. 196–292.

2 Thomas 1994, esp. 265–66.

3 On Clovio's miniature and its relation to the copy by Fröschl, see Simon 1989, illus. pp. 481–82, figs. 39, 40.

4 Ibid., p. 483, illus. p. 482, fig. 41.

5 See ffolliott 1986, pp. 228–29.

6 Ibid., pp. 229–41.

7 On pictorial strategies of presenting Artemisia in Caron's drawings, see ibid., pp. 233–41.

8 Bouvy 1932; French Renaissance in Prints 1994, pp. 147–48, 429–30, no. 172.

9 See Jacobson 1994, p. 150.

10 See European Portrait 1978, p. 148, no. 42.

11 The literature on the representation of Elizabeth is rich. In particular, see Strong 1963; Strong 1987; Yates 1975; Pomeroy 1989; Howarth 1997.

12 See, e.g., the portrait of Richard II in Strong 1987, fig. 20.

13 On portraits of Elizabeth I on government documents see Auerbach 1954, pp. 119–32.

14 On this much-discussed painting, see in particular Jordan 1990.

15 On the importance of Diana in the representation of Elizabeth I, see Strong 1987, pp. 125–28; see also Berry 1989, pp. 62, 64–65.

16 See Strong 1987, pp. 147–48; for a feminist interpretation of the "Mask of Youth" in the context of ageism, see Salomon 1994, pp. 82–90.

17 Kantorowicz 1957; and Bettina Baumgärtel's essay, in this volume.

18 See Kantorowicz 1957, p. 388, n. 245.

19 On this aspect and many other ways of interpreting Judith in images, see Stocker 1998.

20 Davis 1975.

21 On the power of women theme, see Smith 1995. See also Nurse, 1998.

22 See The Prints of Lucas van Leyden, 1983, esp. pp. 102–106.

23 For the oval plaques, see Catalogue of the Painted Enamels 1967, pp. 231–34, nos. 137–38. For the salt cellar, see Baratte 2000, pp. 258–59.

24 On this aspect and others in the Behams' engravings of nudes, see Levy 1988.

25 On images of Judith, and in particular the rarity of nude Judiths, see Zapalac 1994.

26 On ambiguities of the mirror in images of Venus, see Bradshaw and Jones 1983, pp. 44, 47–54; Santore 1997.

27 The classic study of the representation of the heroic woman is Maclean 1977, esp. chap. VII, "Feminist Literature and the Visual Arts," pp. 209–32.

28 On the mixture of heroism and eroticism in this image, see Eva/Ave: Woman in Renaissance and Baroque Prints 1990, pp. 72–73, no. 32.

29 See Maclean 1977, esp. chap. III, "The New Feminism and the Femme Forte, 1630–1650," pp. 64–87.

30 Ibid., pp. 82–86.

31 Discussed in ibid., pp. 220, 222–26.

32 Zafran 1998, pp. 67–71, no. 21, with earlier refs.

33 Cuenin 1987, esp. p. 291; Viennot 1997, pp. 79–96, esp. pp. 85–90.

34 Pariset 1956, pp. 104–111, fig. 8.

35 See Schlumbohm 1978.

36 See Currency of Fame 1994, pp. 350–51, no. 158.

37 On the possible Amazonian reference, see Garrard 1989, pp. 158 and 524, n. 68. Johnson (1999, pp. 115–16) comments on the ambiguity of the nude breast in combination with masculine attributes. For a full analysis of this painting in Rubens's cycle, see Millen and Wolf 1989, pp. 224–27.

38 Berry 1989, pp. 40–41.

39 Tolley (1996, pp. 246–47) notes the use of Juno by French consorts and regents Anne of Brittany, Catherine de' Medici, and Marie de' Medici.

40 Strong 1987, p. 158, figs. 172–73.

41 See Renaissance Medals 1967, p. 105, no. 556; Jones 1982, p. 202, no. 195; and Currency of Fame 1994, pp. 330–31, no. 146a.

42 Jones 1988, pp. 75–76, no. 33.

43 Noted by Jones 1988, pp. 91–92, no. 48.

44 On this painting in the Rubens cycle, see Saward 1982, pp. 142–57; Millen and Wolf 1989, pp. 164–68.

45 On this portrait see Christina, Queen of Sweden 1966, p. 185, no. 352, pl. 20.

46 On this engraving see ibid., p. 186, no. 357.

47 On this title page see ibid., p. 134, nos. 197–98.

48 On this painting, see Anthony van Dyck 1990, pp. 124–26, no. 17.

Opposite: School of Lucas Cranach, Lucretia,
16th century (pl. 17, detail)

Page 180: Jan Muller after Bartholomäus Spranger, Bellona Leading the Armies of the Emperor Against the Turks, 1600 (pl. 86, detail)

Bibliography

David Acton, Hendrik Goltzius and Rudolfine Mannerism in the Graphic Arts, diss., University of Michigan 1994

The Age of Correggio and the Carracci: Emilian Painting of the Sixteenth and Seventeenth Centuries, exhib. cat., ed. Frances P. Smyth et al., Washington, D.C., National Gallery of Art, 1986

The Age of Rubens, exhib. cat. by Peter C. Sutton, Boston, Museum of Fine Arts, 1993

Henricus Cornelius Agrippa, Declamation on the Nobility and Preeminence of the Female Sex, ed. and trans. Albert Rabil, Jr., Chicago (University of Chicago Press) 1996

Albrecht Dürer: Master Printmaker, exhib. cat. by the Department of Prints and Drawings, Boston, Museum of Fine Arts, 1988

Susan Dwyer Amussen, An Ordered Society: Gender and Class in Early Modern England, Oxford (Blackwell) 1988

Susan Dwyer Amussen, "'Being stirred to much unquietness': Violence and Domestic Violence in Early Modern England," Journal of Women's History, VI, 1994, pp. 70–89

Barthélemy Anneau, Emblembuch, 1552

Anthony van Dyck, exhib. cat. by Arthur K. Wheelock, Jr., et al., Washington, D.C., National Gallery of Art, 1990

L'Art en Lorraine au temps de Jacques Callot, exhib. cat. by Jacques Thuillier and Claude Petry-Parisot, Musée des beaux-arts, Nancy, June–September 1992

Erna Auerbach, Tudor Artists: A Study of Painters in the Royal Service and of Portraiture on Illuminated Documents from the Accession of Henry VIII to the Death of Elizabeth I, London (Athlone Press) 1954

Renate Baader, "Heroinen der Literatur: Die französische Salonkultur im 17. Jahrhundert," in Die Galerie der starken Frauen, 1995, pp. 34–50

Simone Berthière, "Le métier de reine en France aux XVIᵉ et XVIIᵉ siècles,"

Mieke Bal, Death and Dissymmetry: The Politics of Coherence in the Book of Judges, Chicago (University of Chicago Press) 1988a

Mieke Bal, Murder and Difference: Gender, Genre, and Scholarship on Sisera's Death, trans. Matthew Gumpert, Bloomington (Indiana University Press) 1988b

Mieke Bal, Reading "Rembrandt": Beyond the Word-Image Opposition, Cambridge (Cambridge University Press) 1991

Mieke Bal, "Head Hunting: 'Judith' on the Cutting Edge of Knowledge," Journal for Studies on the Old Testament, LXIII, 1995, pp. 3–34

Sophie Baratte, Les émaux paints de Limoges, Paris (Réunion des musées nationaux) 2000

Adam Bartsch, Le peintre graveur, 21 vols., Vienna (Degen) 1803–21

Cristelle L. Baskins, "Lucretia: Dangerous Familiars," in Cassone Painting, Humanism, and Gender in Early Modern Italy, Cambridge (Cambridge University Press) 1998, pp. 128–59

Bettina Baumgärtel, "Die Tugendheldin als Symbol kirchlicher und staatlicher Macht" in Die Galerie der starken Frauen 1995, pp. 140–57

Bettina Baumgärtel, "Zum Bilderstreit um die Frau im 17. Jahrhundert: Inszenierungen französischer Regentinnen," Querelles: Jahrbuch für Frauenforschung, II, 1997, pp. 152–82

Pamela Joseph Benson, The Invention of the Renaissance Woman: The Challenge of Female Independence in the Literature and Thought of Italy and England, University Park (Pennsylvania State University Press) 1992

Philippa Berry, Of Chastity and Power: Elizabethan Literature and the Unmarried Queen, London (Routledge) 1989

Simone Berthière, "Le métier de reine en France aux XVIᵉ et XVIIᵉ siècles,"

Proceedings of the Annual Meeting of the Western Society for French History, XXIII, 1996, pp. 1–17

Simone Berthière, "Régence et pouvoir féminin," in Royaume de fémynie: Pouvoirs, contraintes, espaces de liberté des femmes, de la Renaissance à la Fronde, ed. Kathleen Wilson-Chevalier and Eliane Viennot, Paris (Champion) 1999, pp. 63–70

R. Ward Bissell, Orazio Gentileschi and the Poetic Tradition in Caravaggesque Painting, University Park (Pennsylvania State University Press) 1981

Alcuin Blamires, Woman Defamed and Defended: An Anthology of Medieval Texts, New York (Oxford University Press) 1992

Gisela Bock and Margarete Zimmermann, "Die Querelle des femmes in Europa: Eine begriffs- und forschungsgeschichtliche Einführung," Querelles: Jahrbuch für Frauenforschung, II, 1997, pp. 9–38

Jean Bodin, Six Books of a Commonweale, London (Adam Islip) 1606

The Body UnVeiled: Boundaries of the Figure in Early Modern Europe, exhib. cat. by Stephen Campbell and Sandra Seekins, Ann Arbor, University of Michigan Museum of Art, 1997

Lynda E. Boose, "Scolding Brides and Bridling Scolds: Taming the Woman's Unruly Member," Shakespeare Quarterly, XLII, 1991, pp. 179–213

Ruth B. Bottigheimer, "Publishing, Print, and Change in the Image of Eve and the Apple, 1470–1570," Archives for Reformation History, LXXXVI, 1995, pp. 199–235

Eugène Bouvy, "La famille d'Henri IV: A propos d'une estampe de Léonard Gaultier," L'amateur d'estampes, II, no. 6, 1932, pp. 161–76

Jillian Bradshaw and Dorothy M. Jones, "Luxury, Love, and Charity: Four Paintings from the School of

Fontainebleau," Australian Journal of Art, III, 1983, pp. 39–58

Horst Bredekamp, "Die zwei Körper von Thomas Hobbes' Leviathan," in Geschichtskörper: Zur Aktualität von Ernst H. Kantorowicz, ed. Wolfgang Ernst and Cornelia Vismann, Munich (W. Fink) 1998, pp. 105–18.

Horst Bredekamp, Thomas Hobbes visuelle Strategien. Der Leviathan: Urbild des modernen Staates. Werkillustrationen und Portraits, Berlin (Akademie) 1999

Claudia Brink, "Arte et Marte": Kriegskunst und Kunstliebe im Herrscherbild des 15. und 16. Jahrhunderts in Italien (Kunstwissenschaftliche Studien 91), Berlin (Deutscher Kunstverlag) 2000

Judith C. Brown and Robert C. Davis (eds.), Gender and Society in Renaissance Italy, New York (Longman) 1998

Cynthia Burlingham, "Portraiture as Propaganda," in The French Renaissance in Prints from the Bibliothèque nationale de France, exhib. cat., ed. Karen Jacobsen, Los Angeles, New York, and Paris 1995, pp. 139–51

Judith Butler, Bodies That Matter: On the Discursive Limits of "Sex," New York (Routledge) 1993

Eric Josef Carlson, Marriage and the English Reformation, Oxford (Blackwell) 1994

Eugene A. Carroll, "A Drawing by Rosso Fiorentino of Judith and Holofernes," Los Angeles County Museum of Art Bulletin, 1978, pp. 25–49

Baldassare Castiglione, The Book of the Courtier, trans. Charles S. Singleton, Garden City (Doubleday) 1959

Catalogue of the Painted Enamels of the Renaissance, exhib. cat. by Philippe Verdier, Baltimore, Walters Art Museum, 1967

The Cecil Family Collects: Four Centuries of Decorative Arts from Burghley House, exhib. cat. by Oliver Impey, Cincinnati, Cincinnati Art Museum, et al. 1998

Susan P. Cerasano and Marion Wynne-Davies (eds.), Gloriana's Face: Women, Public and Private, in the English Renaissance, Detroit (Wayne State University Press) 1992

Christina, Queen of Sweden—a Personality of European Civilisation, exhib. cat., Stockholm, Nationalmuseum, 1966

Jean Clair, Méduse: Contribution à une anthropologie des arts du visuel, Paris (Gallimard) 1989

Ivan Cloulas, Catherine de Médicis: La passion du pouvoir, Paris (Tallandier) 1999

Sherrill Cohen, The Evolution of Women's Asylums since 1500: From Refuges for Ex-prostitutes to Shelters for Battered Women, Oxford (Oxford University Press) 1992

Fanny Cosandey, "'La blancheur de nos lys': La reine de France au coeur de l'état royal," Revue d'histoire moderne et contemporaine, XLIV, no. 3, 1997, pp. 387–403

Fanny Cosandey, "De lance en quenouille: La place de la reine dans l'Etat moderne (14ᵉ–17ᵉ siècles)," Annales: Histoires, Sciences Sociales, LII, no. 4, July–August 1997, pp. 799–820

Fanny Cosandey, La reine de France: Symbole et pouvoir, XVᵉ–XVIIIᵉ siècle, Paris (Gallimard) 2000

Kathleen Crawford, "Catherine de' Medici and the Performance of Political Motherhood," Sixteenth Century Journal (forthcoming)

Patricia Crawford, Women and Religion in England, 1500–1720, London (Routledge) 1993

Micheline Cuenin, "La Femme and la Guerre (1516–1660)," in Présences féminines: Littérature et société au XVIIᵉ siècle français, ed. Ian Richmond and Constant Venesoen, Paris (Papers on

French Seventeenth Century Literature) 1987, pp. 291–323

Jonathan Culler, Framing the Sign: Criticism and Its Institutions, Norman (University of Oklahoma Press) 1988

The Currency of Fame: Portrait Medals of the Renaissance, exhib. cat., ed. Stephen K. Scher, New York, The Frick Collection, and Washington D.C., the National Gallery of Art, 1994

Hubert Damisch, Le jugement de Pâris, Paris (Flammarion) 1992

Bruce Davis, Master Drawings in the Los Angeles County Museum of Art, Los Angeles (Los Angeles County Museum of Art) 1997

Natalie Zemon Davis, "Women on Top," in Society and Culture in Early Modern France: Eight Essays, ed. Natalie Zemon Davis, Stanford (Stanford University Press) 1975, pp. 124–51

Natalie Zemon Davis, "Boundaries and the Sense of Self in Sixteenth-Century France," in Reconstructing Individualism: Autonomy, Individuality, and the Self in Western Thought, ed. Thomas C. Heller et al., Stanford (Stanford University Press) 1986, pp. 53–63 and 332–35

Natalie Zemon Davis and Arlette Farge (eds.), A History of Women in the West III: Renaissance and Enlightenment Paradoxes, Cambridge MA (Belknap Press) 1993

Holliday T. Day and Hollister Sturges (eds.), Joslyn Art Museum: Paintings and Sculpture from the European and American Collections, Omaha (University of Nebraska Press) 1987

Marie Le Jars de Gournay, L'Egalité des hommes et des femmes [1622], Paris 1989

Christine de Pizan, The Book of the City of Ladies, trans. Earl Jeffrey Richards, New York (Persea) 1982

Frances E. Dolan, Dangerous Familiars: Representations of Domestic Crime in England, 1550–1700, Ithaca (Cornell University Press) 1994

Susan Doran, Monarchy and Matrimony: The Courtships of Elizabeth I, New York (Routledge) 1996

Francis H. Dowley, "French Portraits of Ladies as Minerva," Gazette des Beaux-Arts, XLV, 1955, pp. 261–86

Martha Levine Dunkelman, "The Innocent Salome," Gazette des Beaux-Arts, CXXXIII, 1999, pp. 173–80

Eugène Dutuit, Manuel de l'amateur d'estampes, 6 vols., Amsterdam (G.W. Hissink) 1970–72

Jean Ehrmann, Antoine Caron, peintre de le cour des Valois, 1521–1599, Geneva (Droz) 1955

Jean Ehrmann, Antoine Caron: Peintre des fêtes et des massacres, Paris (Flammarion) 1986

Patricia Emison, "The Singularity of Raphael's Lucretia," Art History, XIV, no. 3, 1991, pp. 372–96

European Paintings of the 16th, 17th, and 18th Centuries: The Cleveland Museum of Art Catalogue of Paintings, Part Three, Cleveland, Cleveland Museum of Art, 1982

European Portraits, 1600–1900, in the Art Institute of Chicago, exhib. cat., ed. Susan Wise, Chicago, Art Institute of Chicago, July–September 1978

Eva/Ave: Woman in Renaissance and Baroque Prints, exhib. cat. by Diane H. Russell with Bernardine Barnes, Washington, D.C., National Gallery of Art, 1990

Christine Fauré, Democracy without Women: Feminism and the Rise of Liberal Individualism in France, trans. Claudia Gorbman and John Berks, Bloomington (Indiana University Press) 1991

Joanna M. Ferraro, "The Power to Decide: Battered Wives in Early Modern Venice," Renaissance Quarterly, III, no. 3, 1995, pp. 493–512

Sheila ffolliott, "Catherine de' Medici as Artemisia: Figuring the Powerful Widow," in Rewriting the Renaissance: The Discourses of Sexual Difference in Early Modern Europe, ed. Margaret W. Ferguson, Maureen Quilligan, and Nancy J. Vickers, Chicago (University of Chicago Press) 1986, pp. 227–41

Sheila ffolliott, "The Ideal Queenly Patron of the Renaissance: Catherine de' Medici Defining Herself or Defined by Others?" in Lawrence 1997, pp. 99–110

Anthony Fletcher, Gender, Sex, and Subordination in England, 1500–1800, New Haven (Yale University Press) 1995

Moderata Fonte (Modesta Pozzo), The Worth of Women: Wherein Is Clearly Revealed Their Nobility and Their Superiority to Men, ed. and trans. Virginia Cox, Chicago (University of Chicago Press) 1997

Louise Olga Fradenburg, ed., Women and Sovereignty, Edinburgh (Edinburgh University Press) 1992

French Master Drawings from the Pierpont Morgan Library, exhib. cat. by Cara Dufour Denison, New York, Pierpont Morgan Library, 1993

The French Renaissance in Prints from the Bibliothèque nationale de France, exhib. cat., ed. Karen Jacobson, Los Angeles, Grunwald Center for the Graphic Arts, University of California, Los Angeles, 1994

From Fontainebleu to the Louvre: French Drawing from the Seventeenth Century, exhib. cat. by Hilliard Goldfarb, Cleveland, Cleveland Museum of Art, 1989

Susan Frye, "The Myth of Elizabeth at Tilbury," Sixteenth Century Journal, XXIII, 1992, pp. 95–114

Susan Frye, Elizabeth I: The Competition for Representation, Oxford (Oxford University Press) 1993

Barbara Gaehtgens, "Macht-Wechsel oder die Übergabe der Regentschaft," in Die Galerie der starken Frauen 1995, pp. 65–78

Die Galerie der starken Frauen – La galerie des femmes fortes: Regentinnen, Amazonen, Salondamen, exhib. cat., ed. Bettina Baumgärtel and Silvia Neysters, Darmstadt, Hessisches Landesmuseum, December–February 1996, Düsseldorf, Kunstmuseum, September–November 1996

Mary D. Garrard, Artemisia Gentileschi: The Image of the Female Hero in Italian Baroque Art, Princeton (Princeton University Press) 1989

Gabriel Gilbert, Semiramis, Paris (Augustin Corbe) 1647

Gods and Heroes: Baroque Images of Antiquity, exhib. cat. by Eunice Williams, New York, Wildenstein Gallery, October 30, 1968–January 4, 1969

Elisabeth Gössmann, "Die Gelehrsamkeit der Frauen im Rahmen der europäischen Querelle des Femmes," in Das Wohlgelahrte Frauenzimmer, ed. Elisabeth Gössman, (Archiv für Philosophie- und theologiegeschichtliche Frauenforschung 1), Munich (Judicium) 1984, pp. 8–20

Laura Gowing, Domestic Dangers: Women, Words, and Sex in Early Modern London, Oxford (Clarendon Press) 1996

Victor E. Graham and W. McAllister Johnson (eds.), The Royal Tour of France by Charles IX and Catherine de' Medici: Festivals and Entries 1564–6, Toronto (University of Toronto Press) 1979

Graven Images: The Rise of Professional Printmakers in Antwerp and Haarlem, 1540–1640, exhib. cat. by Timothy Riggs and Larry Silver, Evanston, Mary and Leigh Block Gallery, Northwestern University, 1993

Janet M. Green, "'I My Self': Queen Elizabeth I's Oration at Tilbury Camp," Sixteenth Century Journal, XXVIII, 1997, pp. 421–45

Stephen J. Greenblatt, Renaissance Self-Fashioning: From More to Shakespeare, Chicago (University of Chicago Press) 1980

Helen Hackett, Virgin Mother, Maiden Queen: Elizabeth I and the Cult of the Virgin Mary, London (Macmillan) 1995

Sarah Hanley, "Engendering the State: Family Formation and State Building in Early Modern France," French Historical Studies, XVI, 1989, pp. 4–27

Sarah Hanley, "Social Sites of Political Practice in France: Lawsuits, Civil Rights, and the Separation of Powers in Domestic and State Government, 1500–1800," American Historical Review, CII, 1997, pp. 27–52

Julie Hardwick, The Practice of Patriarchy: Gender and the Politics of Household Authority in Early Modern France, University Park (Pennsylvania State University Press) 1998

Joel F. Harrington, Reordering Marriage and Society in Reformation Germany, Cambridge (Cambridge University Press) 1995

Mary E. Hazard, "The Case for 'Case' in Reading Elizabethan Portraits," Mosaic, XXIII, 1990, pp. 66–70

Alexander Heidel, The Babylonian Genesis, Chicago (University of Chicago Press) 1942

Katherine Usher Henderson and Barbara F. McManus, Half Humankind: Contexts and Texts of the Controversy about Women in England, 1540–1640, Urbana (University of Illinois Press) 1985

Scott Hendrix, "Masculinity and Patriarchy in Reformation Germany," Journal of the History of Ideas, LVI, 1995, pp. 177–93

Arthur Henkel and Albrecht Schöne (eds.), Emblemata: Handbuch zur Sinnbildkunst des XVI. und XVII. Jahrhunderts, Stuttgart (J. B. Metzler) 1967

A. M. Hind, Engraving in England in the Sixteenth and Seventeenth Centuries: A Descriptive Catalogue with Introductions, 3 vols., Cambridge (Cambridge University Press) 1952–64

F. W. H. Hollstein, Dutch and Flemish Etchings, Engravings, and Woodcuts, ca. 1450–1700, Amsterdam (M. Hertzberger) 1949–

F. W. H. Hollstein, German Engravings, Etchings, and Woodcuts, ca. 1400–1700, Amsterdam (M. Hertzberger) 1954–

Beth L. Holmann, "Goltzius' Great Hercules: Mythology, Art, and Politics," in Nederlands Kunsthistorisch Jaarboek, 42–43, 1991–92, pp. 397–412

Lisa Hopkins, Women Who Would Be Kings: Female Rulers of the Sixteenth Century, New York (St. Martin's) 1991

Murray Hornibrook and Charles Petitjohn, Catalogue of the Engraved Portraits by Jean Morin (c. 1590–1650), Cambridge (Cambridge University Press) 1945

David Howarth, Images of Rule: Art and Politics in the English Renaissance, 1485–1649, Berkeley (University of California Press) 1997

Olwen Hufton, The Prospect Before Her: A History of Women in Western Europe, London (Harper Collins) 1995

Suzanne W. Hull, Women According to Men: The World of Tudor-Stuart Women, Thousand Oaks, CA (Altamira Press) 1996

Margaret Hunt, "Wife Beating, Domesticity, and Women's Independence in Eighteenth-Century London," Gender and History, 4, 1992, pp. 10–29

The Illustrated Bartsch, ed. Walter L. Strauss, New York (Abaris Books) 1978

Mary Jacobus, Reading Women: Essays in Feminist Criticism, New York (Columbia University Press) 1986

Elinor James, Mrs. James Vindication of the Church of England, in an Answer to a Pamphlet Entituled New Test of the Church of England's Loyalty, London 1687

Stephanie Jed, Chaste Thinking: The Rape of Lucretia and the Birth of Humanism, Bloomington (Indiana University Press) 1989

Géraldine A. Johnson, "Imagining Images of Powerful Women: Marie de' Medici's Patronage of Art and Architecture," in Lawrence 1997, pp. 126–53

Géraldine A. Johnson, "Marie de Médicis: Mariée, mère, méduse," in Kathleen Wilson-Chevalier and Eliane Viennot (eds.), Royaume de fémynie: Pouvoirs, contraintes, espaces de liberté des femmes, de la Renaissance à la Fronde, Paris (Champion) 1999, pp. 103–20

Mark Jones, A Catalogue of the French Medals in the British Museum I: 1402–1610, II: 1600–1672, London (British Museum Publications) 1982 (vol. I), 1988 (vol. II)

Constance Jordan, "Representing Political Androgyny: More on the Siena Portrait of Queen Elizabeth I," in The Renaissance Englishwoman in Print: Counterbalancing the Canon, ed. Anne M. Haselkorn and Betty S. Travitsky, Amherst (University of Massachusetts Press) 1990, pp. 157–76

Constance Jordan, Renaissance Feminism: Literary Texts and Political Models, Ithaca (Cornell University Press) 1990

Ernst H. Kantorowicz, The King's Two Bodies: A Study in Mediaeval Political Theology, Princeton (Princeton University Press) 1957

Ernst H. Kantorowicz, Die zwei Körper des Königs: Eine Studie zur politischen Theologie des Mittelalters, 2nd edn., trans. Walter Theimer, Munich (Deutscher Taschenbuch) 1994

Thomas Dacosta Kaufmann, "Empire Triumphant: Notes on an Imperial Allegory by Adriaen de Vries," Studies in the History of Art 8, Washington, D.C. (National Gallery of Art) 1978

Thomas Dacosta Kaufmann, The School of Prague: Painting at the Court of Rudolph II, Chicago (University of Chicago Press) 1988

Hans-Martin Kaulbach, "Weiblicher Frieden—männlicher Krieg? Zur Personifikation des Friedens in der Kunst der Neuzeit," in Allegorie und Geschlechterdifferenz, ed. Inge Stephan and Sigrid Weibel (Studien zur Literatur- und Kulturgeschichte 3), Cologne 1994, pp. 27–49

Joan Kelly, Women, History, and Theory: The Essays of Joan Kelly, Chicago (University of Chicago Press) 1984

John N. King, Tudor Royal Iconography: Literature and Art in an Age of Religious Crisis, Princeton (Princeton University Press) 1989

John N. King, "Queen Elizabeth I: Representations of the Virgin Queen," Renaissance Quarterly XLIII, no. 1, 1990, pp. 30–74

Christiane Klapisch-Zuber, Women, Family, and Ritual in Renaissance Florence, Chicago (University of Chicago Press) 1985

Joan Larsen Klein, ed., Daughters, Wives and Widows: Writings by Men about Women and Marriage in England, 1500–1640, Urbana (University of Illinois Press) 1992

John Knox, The First Blast of the Trumpet against the Monstrous Regiment of Women, Geneva 1558

Jan Piedt Kok, "Hendrick Goltzius—Engraver, Designer, and Publisher, 1582–1600," Nederlands Kunsthistorisch Jaarboek, XLII–XLIII, 1991–92, pp. 159–218

David Kuchta, "The Semiotics of Masculinity in Renaissance England," in Sexuality and Gender in Early Modern Europe: Institutions, Texts, Images, ed. James Grantham Turner, Cambridge (Cambridge University Press) 1993, pp. 233–56

Norman Land, ed., Samuel H. Kress Study Collection at the University of Missouri–Columbia, Columbia (University of Missouri Press) 1999

Gabrielle Langdon, Decorum in Portraits of Medici Women at the Court of Cosimo I, 1537–1574, 2 vols., diss., University of Michigan 1992

Karla Langedijk, The Portraits of the Medici, 15th–18th Centuries, 3 vols., Florence (Studio per Edizioni Scelte) 1981

Cynthia Lawrence, ed., Women and Art in Early Modern Europe: Patrons, Collectors, and Connoisseurs, University Park (Pennsylvania State University Press) 1997

Max Lehrs, Geschichte und kritischer Katalog des deutschen, niederländischen, und französischen Kupferstichs im 15. Jahrhundert, 9 vols., Vienna, 1908–34

Carole Levin, The Heart and Stomach of a King: Elizabeth I and the Politics of Sex and Power, Philadelphia (University of Pennsylvania Press) 1994

Janey L. Levy, "The Erotic Engravings of Sebald and Barthel Beham:

A German Interpretation of a Renaissance Subject," in The World in Miniature 1988, pp. 40–53

Dorothy Limouze, "Aegidius Sadeler, Imperial Printmaker," Bulletin of the Philadelphia Museum of Art, Spring 1989, pp. 2–24

Lust und Verlust: Kölner Sammler zwischen Trikolore und Preussenadler, exhib. cat., ed. Hiltrud Kier and Frank Günter Zehnder, Cologne, Josef-Haubrich-Kunsthalle, October–January 1996

Niccolo Machiavelli, The Prince, [1541] trans. Leo Paul S. de Alvarez, Prospect Heights, IL (Waveland Press) 1980

Ian Maclean, Woman Triumphant: Feminism in French Literature, 1610–1652, Oxford (Clarendon Press) 1977

Ian Maclean, The Renaissance Notion of Woman, Cambridge (Cambridge University Press) 1980

Marie de Medicis et le Palais du Luxembourg, exhib. cat. by M. N. Baudouin-Matuszek et al., Paris, Musée du Luxembourg, 1991

Louis Marin, Le portrait du roi, Paris (Éditions de Minuit) 1981

Lucrezia Marinella, The Nobility and Excellence of Women and the Defects and Vices of Men, ed. and trans. Anne Dunhill, Chicago (University of Chicago Press) 1999

Deborah Marrow, The Art Patronage of Marie de' Medici, Ann Arbor (UMI Research Press) 1982

Megan Matchinske, Writing, Gender, and State in Early Modern England: Identity Formation and the Female Subject, Cambridge (Cambridge University Press) 1998

Peter Matheson, ed. and trans., Argula von Grumbach: A Woman's Voice in the Reformation, Edinburgh (T. & T. Clark) 1995

Franz Matsche, Die Kunst im Dienst der Staatsidee Kaiser Karls VI: Ikonographie, Ikonologie und Programmatik des "Kaiserstils", 2 vols., Berlin (W. de Gruyter) 1981

Sara F. Matthews Grieco, "Querelle des femmes" or "guerre des sexes"? Visual Representations of Women in Renaissance Europe, Florence (European University Institute) 1989

Sara F. Matthews Grieco, Ange ou diablesse: La représentation de la femme au XVIᵉ siècle, Paris (Flammarion) 1991

Elizabeth McGrath, Rubens: Subjects from History II (Corpus Rubenianum Ludwig Burchard 13.1), London (Harvey Miller) 1997

Jeffrey Merrick, "Royal Bees: The Gender Politics of the Beehive in Early Modern Europe," Studies in Eighteenth-Century Culture, XVIII, 1988, pp. 7–37

Jeffrey Merrick, "Fathers and Kings: Patriarchalism and Absolutism in

Eighteenth-Century French Politics," Studies on Voltaire and the Eighteenth Century, CCCVIII, 1993, pp. 281–303

Barbara Hochstetler Meyer, "Marguerite de Navarre and the Androgynous Portrait of François Iᵉʳ," Renaissance Quarterly, IIL, no. 2 (1995), pp. 287–325

Marilyn Migiel and Juliana Schiesari, Refiguring Woman: Perspectives on Gender and the Italian Renaissance, Ithaca (Cornell University Press) 1991

Jodi Mikalachki, The Legacy of Boadicea: Gender and Nation in Early Modern England London (Routledge) 1998

Ronald Forsyth Millen and Robert Erich Wolf, Heroic Deeds and Mystic Figures: A New Reading of Rubens' Life of Maria de' Medici, Princeton (Princeton University Press) 1989

Pavla Miller, Transformations of Patriarchy in the West, 1500–1900, Indiana (Indiana University Press) 1998

The Montreal Museum of Fine Arts: Painting, Sculpture, Decorative Arts, Montreal (Museum of Fine Arts) 1960

Louis Montrose, "Shaping Fantasies: Figurations of Gender and Power in Elizabethan Culture," Representations, 1, 1983, pp. 61–94

Keith Moxey, Peasants, Warriors, and Wives: Popular Imagery in the Reformation, Chicago (University of Chicago Press) 1989

Laura Mulvey, "Visual Pleasure and Narrative Cinema," Screen, XVI, no. 3, 1975, pp. 6–18

Silvia Neysters, "Regentinnen und Amazonen," in Die Galerie der starken Frauen 1995, pp. 99–103

Julia Nurse, "She-Devils, Harlots, and Harridans in Northern Renaissance Prints," History Today, IIL, no. 7, 1998, pp. 41–48

Freeman M. O'Donoghue, A Descriptive and Classified Catalogue of Portraits of Queen Elizabeth, London (Bernard Quaritch) 1894

Karen Offen, European Feminism, 1700–1950: A Political History, Stanford (Stanford University Press) 2000

Old Master Drawings from the Museum of Art, Rhode Island School of Design, exhib. cat. by Deborah J. Johnson, Providence, Rhode Island School of Design Museum of Art, 1983

Susan Gushee O'Malley, ed., Defences of Women: Jane Anger, Rachel Speght, Ester Sowernam, and Constantia Munda (The Early Modern Englishwoman: A Facsimile Library of Essential Works 4.1), New York (Scolar Press) 1996

François-Georges Pariset, "Les Amazones de Claude Deruet," Le Pays Lorrain, XXXVII, 1956, pp. 97–114

Carole Pateman, The Sexual Contract, Stanford (Stanford University Press) 1988

Gustav Pauli, Hans Sebald Beham: Ein kritisches Verzeichnis seiner Kupferstiche, Radierungen, und Holzschnitte [1901–27], Baden-Baden (V. Koerner) 1974

La peinture française du XVIIᵉ siècle dans les collections américaines, exhib. cat. by Pierre Rosenberg, Paris, New York, and Chicago 1982

Mary Elizabeth Perry, Gender and Disorder in Early Modern Seville, Princeton (Princeton University Press) 1990

Peter Paul Rubens, 1577–1640: Eine Ausstellung des Wallraf-Richartz-Museums in der Kunsthalle Köln vom 15. Oktober bis 15. Dezember 1977, II: Maler mit dem Grabstichel. Rubens und die Druckgraphik, exhib. cat., ed. Gerhard Bott et al., Cologne, Museen der Stadt Köln, 1977

Ruprecht Pfeiff, Minerva in der Sphäre des Herrscherbildes: Von der Antike bis zur französischen Revolution, diss., Bonn Universität 1987

Ruprecht Pfeiff, Minerva in der Sphäre des Herrscherbildes: Von der Antike bis zur französischen Revolution (Bonner Studien zur Kunstgeschichte 1), Münster 1990

Hannah Pitkin, Fortune Is a Woman: Gender and Politics in the Thought of Niccolò Machiavelli, Berkeley (University of California Press) 1984

The Political Works of James I, ed. Charles Howard McIlwain, New York (Russell & Russell) 1965

Elizabeth W. Pomeroy, Reading the Portraits of Queen Elizabeth I, Hamden, CT (Archon Books) 1989

The Print in Stuart Britain, 1603–1689, exhib. cat. by Antony Griffiths with the collaboration of Robert A. Gerard, London, British Museum, 1998

Prints and Related Drawings by the Carracci Family: A Catalogue Raisonné, exhib. cat. by Diane DeGrazia Bohlin, Washington, D.C., National Gallery of Art, 1979

The Prints of Lucas van Leyden and His Contemporaries, exhib. cat. by Ellen S. Jacobowitz and Stephanie Loeb Stepanek, Washington, D.C., National Gallery of Art, 1983

Renaissance Medals from the Samuel H. Kress Collection at the National Gallery of Art, Based on the Catalogue of Renaissance Medals in the Gustave Dreyfus Collection, by G. F. Hill, rev. and enlarged by Graham Pollard, London (Phaidon Press) 1967

Cesare Ripa, Iconologia, Milan 1601

A. P. F. Robert-Dumesnil, Le peintre-graveur français, 11 vols., Paris (G. Warée) 1835–71

Gabriel Rollenhagen, Nvclevs emblematvm selectissimorvm, Arnheim 1611

Lyndal Roper, The Holy Household: Women and Morals in Reformation Augsburg, Oxford (Clarendon Press) 1989

Charles M. Rosenberg, "A Drawing by Mathais Zündt, an Engraving by Hans Sebald Beham, and a Seventeenth-Century German Tankard," The University of Michigan Museum of Art Bulletin, V, 1970–71, pp. 18–25

Nanette Salomon, "Positioning Women in Visual Convention: The Case of Elizabeth I," in Attending to Women in Early Modern England, ed. Betty S. Travitsky and Adele F. Seeff, Newark (University of Delaware Press) 1994, pp. 64–95

Rose Marie San Juan, "The Queen's Body and Its Slipping Mask: Contesting Portraits of Queen Christina of Sweden," in ReImagining Women: Representations of Women in Culture, ed. Shirley Neuman and Glennis Stephenson, Toronto (University of Toronto Press) 1993, pp. 19–44

Cathy Santore, "The Tools of Venus," Renaissance Studies, XI, no. 3, 1997, pp. 179–207

Susan Saward, The Golden Age of Marie de' Medici, Ann Arbor (UMI Research Press) 1982

Christa Schlumbohm, "Der Typus der Amazone und das Frauenideal im 17. Jahrhundert: Zur Selbstdarstellung der Grande Mademoiselle," Romanistisches Jahrbuch, IXXX, 1978, pp. 77–99

Christa Schlumbohm, "Die Glorifizierung der Barockfürstin als 'Femme Forte,'" in Europäische Hofkultur im 16. und 17. Jahrhundert, ed. August Buck et al. (Wolfenbütteler Arbeiten zur Barockforschung 9), Hamburg (Hauswedell) 1981, pp. 113–22

Gordon Schochet, Patriarchalism in Political Thought: The Authoritarian Family and Political Speculation and Attitudes, Especially in Seventeenth-Century England, New York (Basic Books) 1975

Sebastian Schütze and Thomas Willette, Massimo Stanzione: L'opera completa, Naples (Electa) 1992

Mary Lyndon Shanley, "Marriage Contract and Social Contract in Seventeenth-Century English Political Thought," in The Family in Political Thought, ed. Jean Bethke Elshtain, Amherst (University of Massachusetts Press) 1982, pp. 80–95, 313–16

Amanda Shephard, Gender and Authority in Sixteenth-Century England: The Knox Debate, Keele (Keele University Press) 1994

Larry Silver and Susan Smith, "Carnal Knowledge: The Late Engravings of Lucas von Leyden," Nederlands

Kunsthistorisch Jaarboek, IXXX, 1978, pp. 239–98

Robert B. Simon, "Giulio Clovio's portrait of Eleonora di Toledo," Burlington Magazine, CXXXI, no. 1036, 1989, pp. 481–85

Hilda L. Smith, ed., Women Writers and the Early Modern British Political Tradition, Cambridge (Cambridge University Press) 1998

Susan L. Smith, The Power of Women: A Topos in Medieval Art and Literature, Philadelphia (University of Pennsylvania Press) 1995

Thomas Smith, De republica Anglorum: The maner of Governement or Policie of the Realme of England, London 1583

Margaret R. Sommerville, Sex and Subjection: Attitudes to Women in Early-Modern Society, London (Arnold) 1995

Lieselotte Steinbrügge, Das moralische Geschlecht: Theorien und literarische Entwürfe über die Natur der Frau in der französischen Aufklärung (Ergebnisse der Frauenforschung 11), Weinheim (Beltz) 1987

Margarita Stocker, Judith, Sexual Warrior: Women and Power in Western Culture, New Haven (Yale University Press) 1998

Roy C. Strong, Portraits of Queen Elizabeth I, Oxford (Clarendon Press) 1963

Roy C. Strong, Gloriana: The Portraits of Queen Elizabeth I, London (Thames and Hudson) 1987

Sustermans: Sessant'anni alla corte dei Medici, exhib. cat., ed. Marco Chiarini and Claudio Pizzorusso, Florence, Palazzo Pitti, July–October 1983

Joseph Swetnam, Female Replies to Swetnam the Woman-Hater: 1615–1620 Editions, introd. Charlie Baxter, London (Thoemmes Press) 1996

Mary Cazort Taylor, European Drawings from the Sonnenschein Collection and Related Drawings in the Collection of the University of Michigan Museum of Art, Ann Arbor (University of Michigan) 1974

Frances Teague, "Elizabeth I: Queen of England," in Women Writers of the Renaissance and Reformation, ed. Katharine M. Wilson, Athens (University of Georgia Press) 1987, pp. 522–47

Marie-Hélène Tesnière and Prosser Gifford (eds.), Creating French Culture: Treasures from the Bibliothèque nationale de France, New Haven (Yale University Press) 1995

Joe A. Thomas, "Fabric and Dress in Bronzino's Portrait of Eleanor of Toledo and Son Giovanni," Zeitschrift für Kunstgeschichte, LVII, no. 2, 1994, pp. 262–67

Paola Tinagli, Women in Italian Renaissance Art: Gender, Representation, Identity, Manchester (Manchester University Press) 1997

Margo Todd, Christian Humanism and the Puritan Social Order, Cambridge (Cambridge University Press) 1987

Toledo Treasures: Selections from the Toledo Museum of Art, New York (Hudson Hills Press) 1995

Thomas Tolley, "States of Independence: Women Regents as Patrons of the Visual Arts in Renaissance France," Renaissance Studies, X, no. 2, 1996, pp. 237–52

W. R. Valentiner, "Joan of Arc by Rubens," North Carolina Museum of Art Bulletin, Fall 1957, pp. 11–16

Eliane Viennot, "Les femmes dans les 'troubles' du XVIᵉ siècle," Clio: Histoire, femmes et sociétés, V, 1997, pp. 79–96

Visions capitales, exhib. cat. by Julia Kristeva, Paris, musée du Louvre, department of graphic arts, April 27–July 27, 1998

Corrado Vivanti, "Henry IV: The Gallic Hercules," Journal of the Warburg and Courtauld Institutes, XXX, 1968, pp. 176–97

Magnus von Platen, ed., Queen Christina of Sweden: Documents and Studies, Stockholm, 1966

C. G. Voorhelm Schneevoogt, Catalogue des estampes gravées d'après P.P. Rubens, Haarlem (Les heritiers Loosjes) 1873

Marina Warner, In Feminine Form: The Embodiment of the True, the Good, and the Beautiful, New York (Atheneum) 1985

Roger-Armand Weigert, Inventaire du fonds français: Graveurs du XVIIᵉ siècle, 5 vols., Paris (Bibliothèque nationale) 1939–68

Merry E. Wiesner, Women and Gender in Early Modern Europe, 2nd. edn., Cambridge (Cambridge University Press), 2000

Joy Wiltenburg, Disorderly Women and Female Power in the Street Literature of Early Modern England and Germany, Charlottesville (University Press of Virginia) 1992

Rudolf Wittkower, Allegorie und der Wandel der Symbole in Antike und Renaissance, Cologne 1984

Linda Woodbridge, Women and the English Renaissance: Literature and the Nature of Womankind, 1540–1620, Urbana (University of Illinois Press) 1984

The World in Miniature: Engravings by the German Little Masters, 1500–1550, exhib. cat., ed. Stephen H. Goddard, Lawrence, Spencer Museum of Art, University of Kansas, 1988

Frances A. Yates, "Queen Elizabeth as Astraea," Journal of the Warburg and Courtauld Institutes, X, 1947, pp. 27–82.

Frances A. Yates, Astraea: The Imperial Theme in the Sixteenth Century, Boston (Routledge) 1975

Eric M. Zafran, French Paintings in the Museum of Fine Arts, Boston I: Artists Born Before 1790, Boston (Museum of Fine Arts) 1998

Kristin E. S. Zapalac, "In His Image and Likeness": Political Iconography and Religious Change in Regensburg, 1500–1600, Ithaca (Cornell University Press) 1990

Kristin E. S. Zapalac, "Judith 'Re-formed,'" in Renaissance, Reform, Reflections in the Age of Dürer, Bruegel, and Rembrandt: Master Prints from the Albion College Collection, ed. Shelley Perlove, Dearborn (University of Michigan, Dearborn) 1994, pp. 57–65

Margarete Zimmermann "Vom Streit der Geschlechte: Die französiche und italienische Querelle des femmes des 15. bis 17. Jahrhunderts," in Die Galerie der starken Frauen 1995, pp. 14–33

Checklist of Works in the Exhibition

The checklist of works refers to the Ann Arbor showing only. All information was accurate at the time of going to press.

I. WIVES AND MOTHERS

Agnolo Bronzino
Italian, 1503–1572
Eleanora of Toledo and Her Son
c. 1545
Oil on panel
121.8 × 100 cm (47⅞ × 39⅜ in.)
Detroit, The Detroit Institute of Arts, Gift of Mrs. Ralph Harman Booth in memory of her husband Ralph Harman Booth
(pl. 51, p. 126)

Justus Sustermans
Flemish, 1597–1681
Maria Maddalena of Austria (Wife of Duke Cosimo II de' Medici) with her Son, the Future Ferdinand II
c. 1623
Oil on canvas
150 × 121.5 cm (58⅜ × 47¾ in.)
Flint, Collection of the Flint Institute of Arts, Gift of Mr. and Mrs. William L. Richards 1965.15
(pl. 52, p. 127)

Daniel Fröschl
German, before 1572–1613
After Giulio Clovio
Italian, born Croatia, 1498–1578
Eleanora of Toledo
c. 1596–1603 (copy of an original of c. 1551–53)
Gouache on vellum
85 × 68 mm (3⅜ × 2¾ in.)
Uffizi Gallery, Florence, Inv. 1890, no. 4186
(not illustrated)

Thomas de Leu
French, c. 1555–c.1612
Portrait of Catherine de' Medici
Late 16th century
Engraving
147 × 98 mm (5⅞ × 3⅞ in.)
sheet, trimmed to platemark
Robert-Dumesnil 332
Lent by the Museum of Fine Arts, Boston, Gift of Gordon Abbott and George P. Gardner
(pl. 53, p. 128)

Guillaume Martin
French, 1558–c. 1590
Portrait of Catherine de' Medici, reverse of medal
1565
Struck silver
37 mm (1½ in.) diam.
Paris, Bibliothèque nationale de France, Médailles, Série royale 162
(pl. 54, p. 129)

Guillaume Dupré
French, c. 1576–c.1643
Christine of Lorraine, Grand Duchess of Tuscany, uniface medal
1609–36
Cast bronze
93 mm (3⅝ in.) diam.
Los Angeles, Los Angeles County Museum of Art, Inv. No. 79.4.183
(pl. 55, p. 130)

Thomas de Leu
French, c. 1555–c. 1612
After François Quesnel
French, 1542/5–1619
Portrait of Henri IV
c. 1600
Engraving
205 × 130 mm (8⅛ × 5⅛ in.)
Robert-Dumesnil 406
Paris, Bibliothèque nationale de France, Hennin 1175
(pl. 49, p. 124)

Thomas de Leu
French, c. 1555–c.1612
After François Quesnel
French, 1542/5–1619
Portrait of Marie de' Medici
c. 1600
Engraving
206 × 139 mm (8⅛ × 5½ in.)
Robert-Dumesnil 455
Paris, Bibliothèque nationale de France, Hennin 1176
(pl. 50, p. 125)

Léonard Gaultier
French, 1561–1641
The Family of Henri IV
1602
Engraving
252 × 312 mm (9⅞ × 12¼ in.)
Weigert 168
Paris, Bibliothèque nationale de France, Hennin 1255
(pl. 59, p. 134)

Léonard Gaultier
French, 1561–1641
After Nicolas Bollery
French, active 1585, died 1630
The Coronation of Marie de' Medici
1610
Engraving
262 × 336 mm (10¼ × 13¼ in.)
Weigert 83
Paris, Bibliothèque nationale de France, Hennin 1358
(pl. 46, p. 115)

Léonard Gaultier
French, 1561–1641
Portrait of Marie de' Medici
1610
Engraving
136 × 80 mm (5⅜ × 3⅛ in.)
Weigert 354
Paris, Bibliothèque nationale de France, Rés. Ed 12g, pet. fol.
(pl. 56, p. 131)

Léonard Gaultier
French, 1561–1641
The Regency of the Queen and Her Prudent Government of the King and Children of France
1613
Engraving
233 × 308 mm (9⅞ × 12⅛ in.) plate, 250 × 323 mm (9⅞ × 12¾ in.) sheet
Weigert 92
Lent by the Museum of Fine Arts, Boston, Purchased from the Harriet Otis Cruft Fund
(pl. 60, p. 135)

Attributed to Jean Warin III
French, c. 1604–1672
Anne of Austria and Her Son, The Future King Louis XIV of France, uniface medallion
1643
Cast, chased, and patinated bronze
94 mm (3¾ in.) diam.
110 mm (4⅜ in.) height including hanging finial
The Art Institute of Chicago, Restricted Gift of Dr. Maxwell Reed Mowry and Mr. and Mrs. George O. Klotter, and the Russell Tyson Fund
(pl. 57, p. 132)

Jean Morin
French, 1605/10–1650
After Philippe de Champaigne
French, 1602–1674
Portrait of Anne of Austria
1645–50
Etching and engraving
300 × 248 mm (11⅞ × 9¾ in.) plate, 471 × 347 mm (18½ × 14⅞ in.) sheet
Robert-Dumesnil 41, Hornibrook and Petitjean 2
National Gallery of Canada, Ottawa, Purchased 1950
(pl. 58, p. 133)

II. THE VIRGIN

Anonymous
16th century
Portrait of Queen Elizabeth I
c. 1559
Oil on panel
36 × 22.8 cm (14 × 9 in.)
Collection of Christopher Foley
(pl. 18, p. 53)

After Nicholas Hilliard
English, c. 1547–1619
Royal Grant showing initial E with miniature of Queen Elizabeth I
1571
Tempera, gold leaf, and ink on vellum, attached by a cord to a bag of hessian cotton inscribed in ink, containing a broken wax seal
45.7 × 66 cm (18 × 26 in.) sheet, 13.9 cm (5½ in.) diam. bag
Stamford, Lincolnshire, The Burghley House Collection
(pl. 62, p. 139)

Before or after George Gower
English, active 1540–1596
Portrait of Queen Elizabeth I
c. 1588
Oil on canvas
101.4 × 97.5 cm (40 × 38¾ in.)
Private collection courtesy of Peter Nahum At The Leicester Galleries
(pl. 63, p. 140)

Anonymous
16th century
Portrait of Queen Elizabeth I
1580s
Agate cameo
23 × 14 mm (1 × ½ in.)
Collection of Christopher Foley
(pl. 64, p. 141)

Anonymous
16th century
The Phoenix Medal, reverse of medal
c.1574
Silver
45 × 41 mm (1¾ × 1⅝ in.)
London, The British Museum,
Department of Coins and Medals
(pl. 66, p. 143)

Anonymous
16th century
Illustration to the *April Eclogue*, folio 11
in Edmund Spenser, *The Shepheardes
Calendar*, London, Hugh Singleton,
1579
Woodcut
60 × 102 mm (2⅜ × 4 in.)
Harry Ransom Humanities Research
Center, The University of Texas at
Austin
(pl. 61, p. 138)

Pieter van der Heyden
Flemish, c. 1530–c.1575
*Queen Elizabeth I and the Pope as Diana
and Callisto*
c. 1585
Engraving
255 × 341 mm (13½ × 10 in.)
O'Donoghue E. 297
London, The British Museum,
Department of Prints and Drawings
(pl. 65, p. 142)

Crispin van de Passe the Elder
Dutch, c. 1565–1637
Portrait of Queen Elizabeth I
1596
Engraving
324 × 254 mm (12¾ × 10 in.)
Hind I, 285
London, The British Museum,
Department of Prints and Drawings
(pl. 20, p. 55)

Crispin van de Passe the Elder
Dutch, c. 1565–1637
After Isaac Oliver
French, active in England,
1558/68–1617
Portrait of Queen Elizabeth I
c. 1603
Engraving
345 × 225 mm (13⅝ × 8⅞ in.)
Hind I, 282–83
Cincinnati, Cincinnati Art Museum,
Bequest of Herbert Greer French
(pl. 19, p. 54)

Francis Delaram
English, c. 1590–1627
After Nicholas Hilliard
English, c. 1547–1619
Portrait of Queen Elizabeth I
c. 1617
Engraving
317 × 221 mm (12½ × 8¾ in.)
Hind II, 219.8
London, The British Museum,
Department of Prints and Drawings
(pl. 2, p. 24)

III. SEDUCTRESSES AND OTHER DANGEROUS WOMEN

Jan Gossaert, called Mabuse
Flemish, c. 1478–1532
Adam and Eve
c. 1525
Black chalk
628 × 460 mm (24¾ × 18⅛ in.)
Providence, The Museum of Art,
Rhode Island School of Design, Walter
H. Kimball Fund, 48.425
(pl. 7, p. 43)

Georg Pencz
German, c. 1500–1550
Samson and Delilah
c. 1531–32
Engraving
39 × 50 mm (1½ × 2 in.)
Bartsch 28
Ann Arbor, University of Michigan
Museum of Art, The W. Hawkins Ferry
Fund, 1999/2.21
(pl. 6, p. 42)

Annibale Carracci
Italian, 1560–1609
Susanna and the Elders
1590
Etching and engraving
333 × 310 mm (13⅛ × 12¼ in.)
Bohlin 14, Bartsch 1
Ann Arbor, University of Michigan
Museum of Art, 1959/1.125
(pl. 35, p. 90)

Giovanni Battista di Jacopo, called
Rosso Fiorentino
Italian, 1494–1540
Judith with the Head of Holofernes
c. 1535–40
Red chalk
232 × 197 mm (9⅛ x7¾ in.)
Los Angeles, Los Angeles County
Museum of Art, Dalzell Hatfield
Memorial Fund, M.77.13
(pl. 34, p. 89)

René Boyvin
French, c. 1530–c.1625
After Giovanni Battista di Jacopo, called
Rosso Fiorentino
Italian, 1494–1540
Judith with the Head of Holofernes
c. 1550–80
Engraving
180 × 130 mm (7⅛ × 5⅛ in.)
Robert-Dumesnil 1
Paris, Bibliothèque nationale de France,
Ed 3 fol., t.2 (R 149199)
(pl. 69, p. 148)

Hans Sebald Beham
German, 1500–1550
After Barthel Beham
German, 1502–1540
Judith Seated in an Arch
1547
Engraving
75 × 50 mm (3 × 2 in.)
Pauli 13
Ann Arbor, University of Michigan
Museum of Art, The W. Hawkins Ferry
Fund, 1998/2.16
(pl. 79, p. 156)

Jerome Wierix
Flemish, c. 1553–1619
After Hans Sebald Beham
German, 1500–1550
Judith Walking to the Left, and Her Servant
1613
Engraving
115 × 73 mm (4½ × 2⅞ in.)
Bartsch 11
Albion, The Albion College Permanent
Print Collection
(pl. 27, p. 82)

Hendrick Goltzius
Dutch, 1558–1617
After Bartholomäus Spranger
Flemish, 1546–1611
Judith with the Head of Holofernes
c. 1585
Engraving
147 mm (5⅞ in.) diam., cut on
borderline
Hollstein 317, Bartsch 272
Lent by the Museum of Fine Arts,
Boston, Harvey D. Parker Collection
(pl. 11, p. 46)

Follower of Bernardino Luini
Italian, c. 1480–c.1532
Salome with the Head of St. John the Baptist
16th century
Oil on canvas
46.6 × 59.7 cm (18½ × 23½ in.)
Cleveland Art Museum, Holden
Collection, 1916.824
(pl. 67, p. 146)

Georg Pencz
German, c. 1500–1550
Tomyris with the Head of Cyrus
c. 1539
Engraving
117 × 73 mm (4¾ × 2⅞ in.) sheet
Bartsch 70
Cambridge, Fogg Art Museum,
Harvard University Art Museums, Gift
of William Gray from the collection of
Francis Calley Gray
(pl. 31, p. 86)

School of Lucas Cranach
German, 1472–1553
Lucretia
16th century
Oil on panel
47 × 34.2 cm (18½ × 13½ in.)
University of California, Berkeley Art
Museum, Bequest of Alfred Bach,
1983.25.6
(pl. 17, p. 52)

Anonymous
German, 17th century
Judith, Venus, and Lucretia, tankard
with cover
1639
Silver, partially gilded, repoussé and
engraved
Height 143 × width 130 × diam.
101 mm (height 5⅝ × width 5⅛ ×
diam. 4 in.) including handle
Ann Arbor, University of Michigan
Museum of Art, 1966/2.18
(pl. 24, p. 79)

Jakob Binck
German, 1500–1569
Or Giovanni Jacopo Caraglio
Italian, c. 1500/05–1565
After Giovanni Battista di Jacopo, called
Rosso Fiorentino
Italian, 1494–1540
Mars and Venus
c. 1530–1540
Engraving
419 × 335 mm (16½ × 13¼ in.)
Bartsch 51
Ann Arbor, University of Michigan
Museum of Art, 1985/1.86
(pl. 70, p. 149)

Guido Reni
Italian, 1575–1642
Venus and Cupid
c. 1626
Oil on canvas
280 × 157 cm (89¾ × 61¾ in.)
Toledo, Toledo Museum of Art,
Purchased with funds from the Libbey
Endowment, Gift of Edward
Drummond Libbey
(pl. 80, p. 157)

Simon Vouet
French, 1590–1649
The Toilette of Venus
c. 1640–45
Oil on canvas
165 × 115 cm (65 × 45¼ in.)
Pittsburgh, Carnegie Museum of Art,
Gift of Mrs. Horace Binney Hare, 1952
(pl. 26, p. 81)

Hendrick Goltzius
Dutch, 1558–1617
Helen of Troy
1615
Oil on canvas
115 × 83.3 cm (45¼ × 32¾ in.)
Lent in honor of Professor Emeritus
Charles Sawyer by a former pupil
(pl. 25, p. 80)

Master MZ (Matthäus Zaisinger?)
German, active c. 1500
Phyllis Riding Aristotle
c. 1500
Engraving
182 × 132 mm (7¼ × 5¼ in.) sheet,
trimmed on platemark
Lehrs 22, Bartsch 18
Lent by the Museum of Fine Arts,
Boston, Stephen Bullard Memorial
Fund and William A. Sargent Fund
(pl. 16, p. 51)

Israhel van Meckenem
Dutch, before 1450–1503
The Angry Wife, from the series *Scenes of
Daily Life*
c. 1495/1503
Engraving
167 × 111 mm (6⅝ × 4⅜ in.)
Lehrs 504
Chapel Hill, Ackland Art Museum, The
University of North Carolina at Chapel
Hill, Ackland Fund
(pl. 15, p. 50)

Lucas van Leyden
Dutch, c. 1494–1533
*Salome taking the Head of St. John the
Baptist to Herodias*, from the series *The
Small Power of Women*
c. 1517
Woodcut
244 × 175 mm (9⅝ × 6⅞ in.) block,
246 × 179 mm (9¾ × 7 in.) sheet
Bartsch 13, Hollstein 22
Lent by the Museum of Fine Arts,
Boston, Gift of Mrs. Lydia Evans
Tunnard in memory of W.G. Russell
Allen
(pl. 68, p. 147)

Dirck Volkertsz. Coornhert
Dutch, 1522–1590
After Maarten van Heemskerck
Dutch, 1498–1574
Jael Slaying Sisera, from *The Power of
Women*, a set of six
1551
Engraving and etching
250 × 195 mm (9⅞ × 7⅝ in.)
Illustrated Bartsch .043.3
Lent by The Metropolitan Museum of
Art, New York, Rogers Fund, 1966
(pl. 38, p. 93)

Dirck Volkertsz. Coornhert
Dutch, 1522–1590
After Maarten van Heemskerck
Dutch, 1498–1574
Samson and Delilah, from *The Power of
Women*, a set of six
1551
Engraving and etching
248 × 197 mm (9¾ × 7¾ in.)
Illustrated Bartsch .043.4
Lent by The Metropolitan Museum of
Art, New York, Rogers Fund, 1966
(pl. 37, p. 92)

Dirck Volkertsz. Coornhert
Dutch, 1522–1590
After Maarten van Heemskerck
Dutch, 1498–1574
Judith Slaying Holofernes, from The Power of Women, a set of six
1551
Engraving and etching
248 × 194 mm (9¾ × 7⅝ in.)
Illustrated Bartsch .043.5
Lent by The Metropolitan Museum of Art, New York, Rogers Fund, 1966
(pl. 28, p. 83)

Dirck Volkertsz. Coornhert
Dutch, 1522–1590
After Maarten van Heemskerck
Dutch, 1498–1574
Solomon's Idolatry, from The Power of Women, a set of six
1551
Engraving and etching
248 × 195 mm (9¾ × 7¾ in.)
Illustrated Bartsch .043.6
Lent by The Metropolitan Museum of Art, New York, Rogers Fund, 1966
(pl. 78, p. 155)

Pierre Reymond
French, c. 1513–after 1584
Solomon Turns to Idolatry, from The Power of Women, a set of six
Third quarter of the 16th century
Painted enamel
292 × 235 mm (11⅝ × 9½ in.)
Baltimore, The Walters Art Museum, Inv. 44.197
(pl. 71, p. 150)

Pierre Reymond
French, c. 1513–after 1584
Jael Kills Sisera, from The Power of Women, a set of six
Third quarter of the 16th century
Painted enamel
292 × 237 mm (11⅝ × 9⅜ in.)
Baltimore, The Walters Art Museum, Inv. 44.200
(pl. 72, p. 150)

Pierre Reymond
French, c. 1513–after 1584
Adam and Eve, from The Power of Women, a set of six
Third quarter of the 16th century
Painted enamel
279 × 222 mm (11 × 8¾ in.)
London, Victoria and Albert Museum, Inv. 8410–1863
(pl. 73, p. 151)

Pierre Reymond
French, c. 1513–after 1584
Lot and His Daughters, from The Power of Women, a set of six
Third quarter of the 16th century
Painted enamel
279 × 222 mm (11 × 8¾ in.)
London, Victoria and Albert Museum, Inv. 8411–1863
(pl. 74, p. 152)

Pierre Reymond
French, c. 1513–after 1584
Samson and Delilah, from The Power of Women, a set of six
Third quarter of the 16th century
Painted enamel
279 × 222 mm (11 × 8¾ in.)
London, Victoria and Albert Museum, Inv. 8412–1863
(pl. 75, p. 152)

Pierre Reymond
French, c. 1513–after 1584
Judith and Holophernes, from The Power of Women, a set of six
Third quarter of the 16th century
Painted enamel
279 × 229 mm (11 × 9 in.)
London, Victoria and Albert Museum, Inv. 8413–1863
(pl. 76, p. 153)

Pierre Reymond
French, c. 1513–after 1584
Hexagonal salt cellar with the Power of Women (*Masculine Weakness*), showing scenes of *The Original Sin, Solomon and the Queen of Sheba, Jael and Sisera, The Fable of Virgil, Samson and Delilah, The Lay of Aristotle*
Mid-16th century
Painted enamel
Height 75 × diam. 93 mm (height 2⅞ × diam. 3⅝ in.)
Paris, Musée du Louvre, Département des Objets d'art, MR R 154
(pl. 77, p. 154)

Aegidius Sadeler
Flemish, 1570–1629
After Bartholomäus Spranger
Flemish, 1546–1611
Hercules and Omphale
Mid-1590s
Etching and engraving
431 × 316 mm (17 × 17½ in.) sheet
Illustrated Bartsch .105, Hollstein 106
Lent by The Metropolitan Museum of Art, New York, Harris Brisbane Dick Fund, 1953
(not illustrated)

Michel Dorigny
French, 1617–1665
After Simon Vouet
French, 1590–1649
Hercules and Omphale
1643
Engraving with etching
217 × 159 mm (8½ × 6⅜ in.)
Weigert 90
Paris, Bibliothèque nationale de France, Sa 37 fol. (M 57897)
(pl. 44, p. 114)

IV. THE HEROINE

Albrecht Dürer
German, 1471–1528
The Annunciation, from The Life of the Virgin
c. 1503
Woodcut
295 × 212 mm (11⅝ in. × 8⅜ in.)
Bartsch 83
Ann Arbor, University of Michigan Museum of Art, Gift of the Friends of the Museum in memory of Helen B. Hall, Curator Emeritus, 1992/1.125
(pl. 81, p. 160)

Massimo Stanzione
Italian, 1585–1656
Susanna and the Elders
1631–37
Oil on canvas
158 × 178.6 cm (60 × 70¼ in.)
Joslyn Art Museum, Omaha, Museum purchase
(pl. 36, p. 91)

Fede Galizia
Italian, c. 1578–1630
Judith with the Head of Holofernes
1596
Oil on canvas
120.5 × 94 cm (47½ × 37 in.)
Gift of Mr. and Mrs. Jacob Polak, The John and Mable Ringling Museum of Art, Sarasota
(pl. 32, p. 87)

Cornelis Galle the Elder
Flemish, 1576–1650
After Peter Paul Rubens
Flemish, 1577–1640
Judith Beheading Holofernes
c. 1610
Engraving
550 × 380 mm (21⅝ × 15 in.)
Hollstein 31
Lent by The Metropolitan Museum of Art, New York, The Elisha Whittelsey Collection, The Elisha Whittelsey Fund, 1951
(pl. 82, p. 161)

Elisabetta Sirani
Italian, 1638–1665
Judith
c. 1662
Oil on canvas
124.5 × 162.8 cm (49 × 64 in.)
University Art Museum, University of California, Santa Barbara, Gift of Gary C. Gallup
(pl. 30, p. 85)

Marcantonio Raimondi
Italian, 1480–1527/34
After Raphael
Italian, 1483–1520
Death of Lucretia
c. 1511–12
Engraving
214 × 134 mm (8½ × 5¼ in.) sheet, trimmed on platemark
Bartsch 192
Lent by the Museum of Fine Arts, Boston, Gift of Mrs. T. Jefferson Coolidge
(pl. 39, p. 94)

Paulus Pontius
Flemish, 1603–1658
After Peter Paul Rubens
Flemish, 1577–1640
The Head of Cyrus Brought to Queen Tomyris
1630
Engraving
403 × 588 mm (15⅞ × 23⅛ in.)
plate, 410 × 515 mm (16⅛ × 23½ in.) sheet
Dutuit 22, Hollstein 40
Lent by the Museum of Fine Arts, Boston, Stephen Bullard Memorial Fund
(pl. 33, p. 88)

François Chauveau
French, 1613–1676
Tomyris, in Jacques Du Bosc, La femme héroïque, ou, Les héroïnes comparées avec les héros en toutes sortes de vertus. Et plusieurs reflexions morales à la fin de chaque comparaison, Paris, Antoine de Sommaville and Augustin Courbé, 1645
Engraving
180 × 125 mm (7 × 5 in.) image
Saint Bonaventure, Saint Bonaventure University, Friedsam Memorial Library, Franciscan Institute Collection
(pl. 9, p. 44)

Aegid Rousselet
French, n.d.
and Abraham Bosse
French, 1602–1676
After Claude Vignon
French, 1593–1670
Zenobia, in Pierre Le Moyne, La Gallerie des femmes fortes, Paris, Antoine de Sommaville, 1647
Engraving with etching
340 × 215 mm (13⅜ × 8⅜ in.)
New Haven, The Beinecke Rare Book and Manuscript Library, Yale University
(pl. 13, p. 48)

Paulus Moreelse
Dutch, 1571–1638
Death of Lucretia
1612
Woodcut
257 × 329 mm (10⅛ × 13 in.)
Hollstein 1
Ann Arbor, University of Michigan Museum of Art, 1959/1.127
(pl. 40, p. 95)

Georg Pencz
German, c. 1500–1550
Artemisia Preparing to Drink Her Husband's Ashes
c. 1539
Engraving
191 × 135 mm (7½ × 5⅜ in.)
Illustrated Bartsch 83 (343)
San Francisco, Fine Art Museums of San Francisco, Achenbach Foundation for Graphic Arts
(pl. 42, p. 112)

Gerrit van Honthorst
Dutch, 1592–1656
Artemisia
1632–35
Oil on canvas
170 × 147.5 cm (67 × 58 in.)
Princeton, The Art Museum, Princeton University, Museum purchase, gift of George L. Craig, Class of 1921, and Mrs. Craig
(pl. 43, p. 113)

V. THE WARRIOR WOMAN

Antonio Tempesta
Italian, 1555–1630
Judith and Holofernes, from Biblical Battles
1613
Etching
206 × 284 mm (8⅛ × 11⅛ in.) plate
Bartsch 258
Cambridge, Fogg Art Museum, Harvard University Art Museums, Gift of Melvin R. Seiden
(pl. 29, p. 84)

Paris Bordone
Italian, 1500–1571
Athena Scorning the Advances of Hephaestus
c. 1555–60
Oil on canvas
139.4 × 127.7 cm (54⅞ × 50¼ in.)
Columbia, Museum of Art and Archaeology, University of Missouri-Columbia, Gift of the Samuel H. Kress Foundation
(pl. 12, p. 47)

Jan Muller
Dutch, 1571–1628
After Bartholomäus Spranger
Flemish, 1546–1611
Bellona Leading the Armies of the Emperor
Against the Turks
1600
Engraving
704 × 510 mm (27¾ × 20 in.)
Hollstein 50, Illustrated Bartsch 75
Minneapolis, Lent by The Minneapolis
Institute of Arts, The Ethel Morrison
Van Derlip Fund
(pl. 86, p. 166)

Aegidius Sadeler
Flemish, 1570–1629
After Bartholomäus Spranger
Flemish, 1546–1611
The Triumph of Wisdom over Ignorance
c. 1600
Engraving
508 × 358 mm (20 × 14⅛ in.)
Hollstein 115
Chapel Hill, Ackland Art Museum, The
University of North Carolina at Chapel
Hill, Ackland Fund
(pl. 87, p. 167)

Jacques Jonghelinck (Jongeling)
Flemish, 1530–1606
Margaret of Austria, Duchess of Parma, as
an allegorical figure in classical garments,
reverse of medal
1559–67
Cast silver
595 mm (2⅜ in.) diam.
Brussels, Royal Library of Belgium,
Coins and Medals
(pl. 85, p. 165)

Thomas Cecil
English, active c. 1625–1640
Truth Presents the Queen with a Lance
c. 1625
Engraving
273 × 299 mm (10¾ × 11¾ in.)
O'Donoghue E. 287
London, The British Museum,
Department of Prints and Drawings
(pl. 3, p. 25)

Attributed to Peter Paul Rubens
Flemish, 1577–1640
Joan of Arc
c. 1618–20
Oil on canvas
181.8 × 116.3 cm (71½ × 45¾ in.)
Raleigh, North Carolina Museum of
Art, Raleigh, Purchased with funds
from the State of North Carolina and
the North Carolina Art Society, Robert
F. Phifer Bequest
(pl. 83, p. 163)

Jean-Baptiste Massé
French, 1687–1767
After Peter Paul Rubens
Flemish, 1577–1640
Marie de' Medici as Minerva
1708?
Engraving
510 × 358 mm (20 × 14 in.) plate,
682 × 502 mm (26⅞ × 19¾ in.)
sheet
Voorhelm Schneevoogt 220, 19.1
Lent by The Metropolitan Museum of
Art, New York, Gift of Georgiana W.
Sargent, in memory of John Osborne
Sargent, 1924
(pl. 22, p. 58)

Grégoire Huret
French, 1606–1670
Blanche of Castile as Minerva, title page in
Charles Combault d'Auteuil, Blanche
infante de Castille, mère de S. Louis....,
Paris, Antoine de Sommaville, 1644
Engraving
220 × 160 mm (8⅝ × 6¼ in.)
Cambridge, Harvard University,
Houghton Library
(pl. 1, p. 23)

Claude Deruet
French, c. 1588–1660
Departure of the Amazons, from a cycle of
Battles of the Amazons
1620s
Oil on canvas
50.8 × 66 cm (20 × 26 in.)
Lent by The Metropolitan Museum of
Art, New York, Bequest of Harry G.
Sperling, 1971
(pl. 4, p. 40)

Claude Deruet
French, c. 1588–1660
Triumph of the Amazons, from a cycle of
Battles of the Amazons
1620s
Oil on canvas
51.4 × 66 cm (20¼ × 26 in.)
Lent by The Metropolitan Museum of
Art, New York, Bequest of Harry G.
Sperling, 1971
(pl. 5, p. 41)

Laurent de la Hyre
French, 1606–1656
Tancred and Clorinda, a scene from
Torquato Tasso, La Gerusalemme Liberata
Before 1630
Black and white chalk
292 × 400 mm (11½ × 15¾ in.)
Ann Arbor, University of Michigan
Museum of Art, Purchased from the
Estate of Edward Sonnenschein,
1970/2.88
(pl. 84, pp. 164–65)

VI. THE GODDESS

Attributed to Jean de Court
French, active 1572–1585
Portrait of Henri IV and The Triumph of
Venus, salt cellar
Early 17th century
Enamel
Height 80 × diam. 90 mm
(height 3⅛ × diam. 3½ in.)
Angers, Musées d'Angers
(pl. 90, p. 172)

Attributed to Jean de Court
French, active 1572–1585
Portrait of Marie de' Medici and The
Triumph of Diana, salt cellar
Early 17th century
Enamel
Height 80 × diam. 90 mm
(height 3⅛ × diam. 3½ in.)
Angers, Musées d'Angers
(pl. 91, p. 172)

Attributed to Matthieu Jacquet
French, c. 1545–1611
Marie de' Medici as Juno
c. 1600?
Bronze
Height 48.5 × width 30 cm
(height 19⅛ × width 11⅞ in.)
Baltimore, The Walters Art Museum,
Inv. 54.668
(pl. 89, p. 171)

Nicolas Briot
French, 1605–1646
Marie de' Medici as Juno on a rainbow with
the fleur-de-lis of France, reverse of medal
1613
Struck silver
52 mm (2⅛ in.) diam.
Paris, Bibliothèque nationale de France,
Médailles, Série royale 379
(pl. 92, p. 173)

Guillaume Dupré
French, c. 1576–1643
Louis XIII as Dauphin between Henri IV as
Mars and Marie de' Medici as Minerva,
reverse of medal
1603
Gilt bronze
68 mm (2¾ in.) diam., with loop
National Gallery of Art, Washington,
Samuel H. Kress Collection
1957.14.1151a
(pl. 41, p. 111)

Attributed to Philippe Danfrie the
Younger
French, c. 1572–1604
Henri IV as Mars and Marie de' Medici as
Minerva, reverse of medal
1604
Struck silver
56 mm (2¼ in.) diam.
Los Angeles, Los Angeles County
Museum of Art, Inv. No. 79.4.128
(pl. 93, p. 174)

Guillaume Dupré
French, c. 1576–1643
Louis XIII as Apollo and Marie de' Medici
as Minerva, reverse of medal
1611
Cast silver
49 mm (2 in.) diam.
London, The British Museum,
Department of Coins and Medals,
M2250
(pl. 95, p. 175)

Alexis Loir
French, 1640–1713
After Jean-Marc Nattier
French, 1685–1766
After Peter Paul Rubens
Flemish, 1577–1640
The Education of the Queen
c. 1704–08
Engraving
445 × 337 mm (17½ × 13¼ in.)
Voorhelm Schneevoogt 220, 19.6
Kunstmuseum Düsseldorf, Graphische
Sammlung, Inv. Nr. KA (FP) 10954 D
(pl. 88, p. 170)

Thomas de Leu
French, c. 1555–c.1612
After Isaïe Fournier
French, 17th century
Portrait of Marie de' Medici as Justice
1609
Engraving
198 × 144 mm (7¾ × 5⅝ in.) plate
Robert-Dumesnil 456
Cambridge, Fogg Art Museum,
Harvard University Art Museums,
Jakob Rosenberg Fund
(pl. 47, p. 116)

Bernard Picard
French, 1673–1733
After Jean-Marc Nattier
French, 1685–1766
After Peter Paul Rubens
Flemish, 1577–1640
The Felicity of the Regency, 1704, in
La Gallerie du Palais du Luxembourg...,
Paris, Duchange, 1710
Engraving
500 × 355 mm (19⅝ × 14 in.) plate
Voorhelm Schneevoogt 220, 19.18
New York, The New York Public
Library
(pl. 23, p. 59)

Guillaume Dupré
French, c. 1576–1643
Marie de' Medici as Cybele, reverse of
medal
1615
Cast bronze
62 mm (2½ in.) diam.
London, Victoria and Albert Museum,
A.358-1910 (Salting Bequest)
(pl. 96, p. 176)

Antoine Trouvain
French, 1656–1708
After Jean-Baptiste Nattier
French, 1678–1726
After Peter Paul Rubens
Flemish, 1577–1640
The Majority of Louis XIII
c. 1704–08
Engraving
442 × 339 mm (17⅜ × 13⅜ in.)
Voorhelm Schneevoogt 220, 19.19
Washington, Smithsonian Institution
National Museum of American History,
Behring Center
(pl. 97, p. 176)

Guillaume Dupré
French, c. 1576–1643
Marie de' Medici as mother of the gods,
reverse of medal
1624
Bronze
54 mm (2⅛ in.) diam.
National Gallery of Art, Washington,
Samuel H. Kress Collection
1957.14.1162a
(pl. 94, p. 174)

Jeremias Falck
Polish, c. 1610
After David Beck
Dutch, c. 1621–1656
And Erasmus Quellinus
Flemish, c. 1607–1678
Christina of Sweden as Minerva
1649
Engraving
350 × 224 mm (13⅞ × 9 in.)
Hollstein 221
Kunstmuseum Düsseldorf, Graphische
Sammlung, Inv. Nr. KA (FP) 23728 D
(pl. 98, p. 177)

Jeremias Falck
Polish, c. 1610
After Sébastien Bourdon
French, 1616–1671
Christina receives the Herculean Arms from
Gustav II Adolf, as Fame Records Swedish
Victory in Germany, title page to Bogislav
Philipp von Chemnitz, Koeniglichen
Schwedischen in Teutschland gefuehrten
Krieges..., vol. 2, Stockholm, J.
Janssonius, 1653
Engraving
178 × 280 mm (7 × 11 in.)
New Haven, The Beinecke Rare Book
and Manuscript Library, Yale
University
(pl. 48, p. 117)

After Niccolò dell'Abate
Italian, 1509/12–1571
Portrait of François I
16th century
Engraving
277 × 190 mm (10⅞ × 7½ in.)
Paris, Bibliothèque nationale de France,
N2 François Ier (D145211)
(pl. 45, p. 114)

Photographic Credits

PLATES

1: Houghton Library, Harvard University; 2: © The British Museum; 3: © The British Museum; 4: Photograph © 1991 The Metropolitan Museum of Art; 5: Photograph © 1991 The Metropolitan Museum of Art; 6: Ann Arbor, University of Michigan Museum of Art, The W. Hawkins Ferry Fund, 1999/2.21; 7: Museum of Art, Rhode Island School of Design, Walter H. Kimball Fund: Photography by Erik Gould; 8, 9, 10: Saint Bonaventure University. Franciscan Institute Collection; 11: Harvey D. Parker Collection, P7282. Courtesy, Museum of Fine Arts, Boston. Reproduced with permission. © 2000 Museum of Fine Arts, Boston. All Rights Reserved.; 12: Museum of Art and Archaeology, University of Missouri-Columbia, Gift of the Samuel H. Kress Foundation; 13: The Beinecke Rare Book and Manuscript Library, Yale University; 14: The Beinecke Rare Book and Manuscript Library, Yale University; 15: Ackland Art Museum, The University of North Carolina at Chapel Hill, Ackland Fund; 16: Stephen Bullard Memorial Fund and William A. Sargent Fund, 53.122. Courtesy, Museum of Fine Arts, Boston. Reproduced with permission. © 2000 Museum of Fine Arts, Boston. All Rights Reserved.; 17: University of California Berkeley Art Museum; Bequest of Alfred Bach. Photographed for the UC Berkeley Art Museum by Benjamin Blackwell; 18: Courtesy of Christopher Foley; 19: Cincinnati Art Museum, Bequest of Herbert Greer French, 1942; 20: © The British Museum; 21: Courtesy of the Fogg Art Museum, Harvard University Art Museums, Gift of Mr. and Mrs. Winslow Ames. Photo credit: Katya Kallsen, © Harvard University; 22: The Metropolitan Museum of Art, Gift of Georgiana W. Sargent in memory of John Osborn Sargent, 1924 (24.63.1037); 23: Spencer Collection, The New York Public Library, Astor, Lenox and Tilden Foundations; 24: Ann Arbor, University of Michigan Museum of Art, 1966/2.18; 25: Private collection; 26: Carnegie Museum of Art, Pittsburgh, Gift of Mrs. Horace Binney Hare. Photo credit: Peter Harholdt; 27: Collection of Albion College; 28: The Metropolitan Museum of Art, Rogers Fund, 1966 (66.602.17); 29: Courtesy of the Fogg Art Museum, Harvard University Art Museums, Gift of Melvin R. Seiden. Photo credit: Katya Kallsen, © Harvard University; 30: University Art Museum, University of California, Santa Barbara, Gift of Gary C. Gallup; 31: Courtesy of the Fogg Art Museum, Harvard University Art Museums, Gift of William Gray from the collection of Francis Calley Gray. Photo credit: Katya Kallsen, © Harvard University; 32: Gift of Mr. and Mrs. Jacob Polak, Collection of The John and Mable Ringling Museum of Art, the State Art Museum of Florida; 33: Stephen Bullard Memorial Fund, 1978.60. Courtesy, Museum of Fine Arts, Boston. Reproduced with permission. © 2000 Museum of Fine Arts, Boston. All Rights Reserved.; 34: Los Angeles County Museum of Art, Dalzell Hatfield Memorial Fund. © 2001 Museum Associates/LACMA; 35: Ann Arbor, University of Michigan Museum of Art, 1959 / 1.125; 36: Joslyn Art Museum, Omaha, Nebraska; 37: The Metropolitan Museum of Art, Rogers Fund, 1966 (66.602.14); 38: The Metropolitan Museum of Art, Rogers Fund, 1966 (66.602.13); 39: Gift of Mrs. T. Jefferson Coolidge, 21.10894. Courtesy, Museum of Fine Arts, Boston. Reproduced with permission. © 2000 Museum of Fine Arts, Boston. All Rights Reserved.; 40: Ann Arbor, University of Michigan Museum of Art, 1959/1.127; 41: Samuel H. Kress Collection, Photograph © 2001 Board of Trustees, National Gallery of Art, Washington; 42: Fine Arts Museums of San Francisco, Achenbach Foundation for the Graphic Arts, 1963.30.756; 43: The Art Museum, Princeton University. Museum purchase, with funds given by George L. Craig, Jr., Class of 1921, and Mrs. Craig. Photo credit: Bruce M. White, y1968–117; 44: Paris, Bibliothèque nationale de France; 45: Bibliothèque nationale de France; 46: Bibliothèque nationale de France; 47: Courtesy of the Fogg Art Museum, Harvard University Art Museums, Jakob Rosenberg Fund. Photo credit: Katya Kallsen, © Harvard University; 48: The Beinecke Rare Book and Manuscript Library, Yale University; 49: Bibliothèque nationale de France; 50: Bibliothèque nationale de France; 51: Gift of Mrs. Ralph Harman Booth in memory of her husband Ralph Harman Booth. Photograph © 1994 The Detroit Institute of Arts; 52: Collection of the Flint Institute of Arts, Gift of Mr. and Mrs. William L. Richards, 1965.15; 53: Gift of Gordon Abbott and George P. Gardner, M28940. Courtesy, Museum of Fine Arts, Boston. Reproduced with permission. © 2000 Museum of Fine Arts, Boston. All Rights Reserved.; 54: Bibliothèque nationale de France; 55: Los Angeles County Museum of Art, Purchased with funds provided by Mr. and Mrs. Alfred Hart. Photograph ©2001 Museum Associates/LACMA; 56: Bibliothèque nationale de France; 57: Mr. Michael Hall, New York. Russell Tyson Restricted Gift. Maxwell Reed Mowry Restricted Gift. Mr. and Mrs. George O. Klotter Restricted Gift. 1977.494 The Art Institute of Chicago. All Rights Reserved.; 58: National Gallery of Canada, Ottawa, Purchased 1950; 59: Bibliothèque nationale de France; 60: Purchased from the Harriet Otis Cruft Fund, M28435. Courtesy, Museum of Fine Arts, Boston. Reproduced with permission. © 2000 Museum of Fine Arts, Boston. All Rights Reserved.; 61: Harry Ransom Humanities Research Center, The University of Texas at Austin; 62: The Burghley House Collection; 63: The Leicester Galleries; 64: Collection of Christopher Foley; 65: © The British Museum; 66: © The British Museum; 67: © The Cleveland Museum of Art, Holden Collection, 1916.824; 68: Gift of Mrs. Lydia Evans Tunnard in memory of W. G. Russell Allen, 66.1082. Courtesy, Museum of Fine Arts, Boston. Reproduced with permission. © 2000 Museum of Fine Arts, Boston. All Rights Reserved.; 69: Bibliothèque nationale de France; 70: Ann Arbor, University of Michigan Museum of Art, 1985/1.86; 71: The Walters Art Museum, Baltimore; 72: The Walters Art Museum, Baltimore; 73: V&A Picture Library; 74: V&A Picture Library; 75: V&A Picture Library; 76: V&A Picture Library; 77: Réunion des Musées Nationaux / Art Resource, NY; 78: The Metropolitan Museum of Art, Rogers Fund, 1966 (66.548.26); 79: Ann Arbor, University of Michigan Museum of Art, The W. Hawkins Ferry Fund, 1998/2.16; 80: Toledo Museum of Art; Toledo, Ohio; Purchased with funds from the Libbey Endowment, Gift of Edward Drummond Libbey, acc.no.1972.86; 81: Ann Arbor, University of Michigan Museum of Art, 1992/1.125; 82: The Metropolitan Museum of Art, The Elisha Whittelsey Collection, The Elisha Whittelsey Fund, 1951 (51.501.7000); 83: North Carolina Museum of Art, Raleigh, Purchased with funds from the State of North Carolina and the North Carolina Art Society (Robert F. Phifer Bequest); 84: Ann Arbor, University of Michigan Museum of Art, Purchased from the Estate of Edward Sonnenschein, 1970/2.88; 85: Bibliothèque royale de Belgique, Cabinet des Médailles; 86: The Minneapolis Institute of Arts; 87: Ackland Art Museum, The University of North Carolina at Chapel Hill, Ackland Fund; 88: Düsseldorf, museum kunst palast, Sammlung der Kunstakademie (NRW), Inv. KA (FP) 10954D; 89: The Walters Art Museum, Baltimore; 90: Cliché Musées d'Angers; 91: Cliché Musées d'Angers; 92: Bibliothèque nationale de France; 93: Los Angeles County Museum of Art, Purchased with funds provided by Mrs. Maria F. K. Fliermans in memory of Constantinia Fliermans, Jr. Photograph © 2001 Museum Associates/LACMA; 94: Samuel H. Kress Collection, Photograph © 2001 Board of Trustees, National Gallery of Art, Washington; 95: © The British Museum; 96: The Metropolitan Museum of Art, Gift of James Hazen Hyde, 1948. (48.90.7); 97: Graphic Arts Collection, National Museum of American History, Smithsonian Institution, Photograph number: 2001–7515; 98: Düsseldorf, museum kunst palast, Sammlung der Kunstakademie (NRW), Inv. KA (FP) 23728 D

FIGURES

1: © Christie's Images New York; 2: Museen der Stadt Nürnberg; 3: The Pierpont Morgan Library, New York 1955.7; 4: Kunstsammlungen der Veste Coburg, Germany; 5: Spencer Museum of Art: Museum Purchase; 6: Photograph © 1988 The Metropolitan Museum of Art; 7: © Bildarchiv Preussischer Kulturbesitz, Berlin 2001, Staatliche Museen zu Berlin.: Photo: Jorg P. Anders; 8: Copyright Scala / Art Resource, NY. Uffizi, Florence, Italy; 9: Archivio Fotografico Soprintendenza Beni Artistici e Storici di Roma; 10: Museum Boijmans Van Beuningen, Rotterdam; 11: Rijksmuseum Amsterdam; 12: Photograph © 2001 Board of Trustees, National Gallery of Art, Washington DC; 13: The Minneapolis Institute of Arts; 14: Montreal Museum of Fine Arts, Gift of Mrs. F. Cleveland Morgan.: Photo: The Montreal Museum of Fine Arts; 15: The Toledo Museum of Art, Toledo, Ohio; 16: Staatsgalerie Stuttgart; 17: © Bildarchiv Preussischer Kulturbesitz, Berlin 2001, Staatliche Museen zu Berlin.: Photo: Jorg P. Anders; 18: Wadsworth Atheneum, Hartford, Connecticut; 19: The Beinecke Rare Book and Manuscript Library, Yale University; 20: Bibliothèque nationale de France; 21: Bibliothèque nationale de France; 22: Paris, Musée du Louvre; 23: © Stadtmuseum Münster, Photo: Tomasz Samek; 24: Rijksmuseum, Amsterdam; 25: Rijksmuseum, Amsterdam; 26: Düsseldorf, Heinrich-Heine-Institut; 27: Réunion des Musées Nationaux; 28: The Royal Collection © 2001, Her Majesty Queen Elizabeth II; 29: Photo credit: © Jean-Louis Boutillier, Amiens; 30: Su concessione del Ministero per i Beni e le Attività Culturali—Soprintendenza per il Patrimonio Storico Artistico e Demoetnoantropologico di Siena; 31: Rijksmuseum Amsterdam; 32: Albertina, Wien; 33: M. Theresa B. Hopkins Fund, 48.16. Courtesy, Museum of Fine Arts, Boston. Reproduced with permission. © 2000 Museum of Fine Arts, Boston. All Rights Reserved.; 34: Photo: The National Museum of Art, Stockholm; 35: Derek Johns Ltd., London

Index